# Contents

Left: a bronze figure of a Roman soldier, dated about A.D. 150. Armies of brave, well-disciplined men like this built the vast Roman Empire. In so doing, they discovered, explored, and settled lands in Europe, Asia, and Africa previously unknown to the civilized world around the Mediterranean.

Frontispiece: an artist's impression of Neanderthal people roaming through rugged country. Migrating tribes of prehistoric men had made their way across all the continents except Antarctica before civilization really began in about 4000 B.C. These tribes were the true "first explorers."

# List of Maps

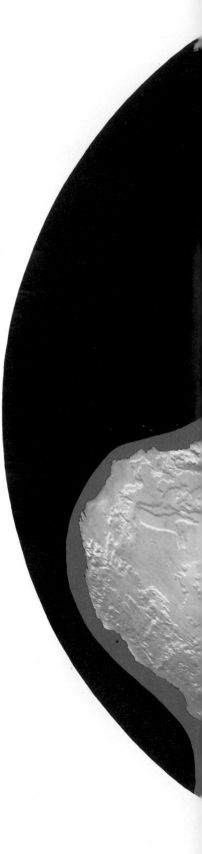

The illuminated globe highlights in
blue the areas of the world discovered
and explored by the peoples of the
ancient world. It shows how the men
of each successive civilization—
Egypt, Phoenicia, Greece, Carthage,
and Rome—spread wider and wider
the frontiers of the known world.
Sailing, riding, and marching, they
pushed north to Iceland, south around
Africa, and eastward across the vast
deserts and mountain ranges of Asia.

# THE FIRST EXPLORERS

## BY FELIX BARKER
in collaboration with Anthea Barker

Executive Coordinators: Beppie Harrison
                       John Mason

Design Director: Guenther Radtke

Editorial: Mary Senechal
           Gail Roberts
           Damian Grint

Picture Editor: Peter Cook

Research: Ann Reading

Cartography by Geographical Projects

This edition specially produced in 1973
for International Learning Systems
Corporation Limited, London
by Aldus Books Limited, London.

Printed and bound in Yugoslavia by
Mladinska Knjiga, Ljubljana

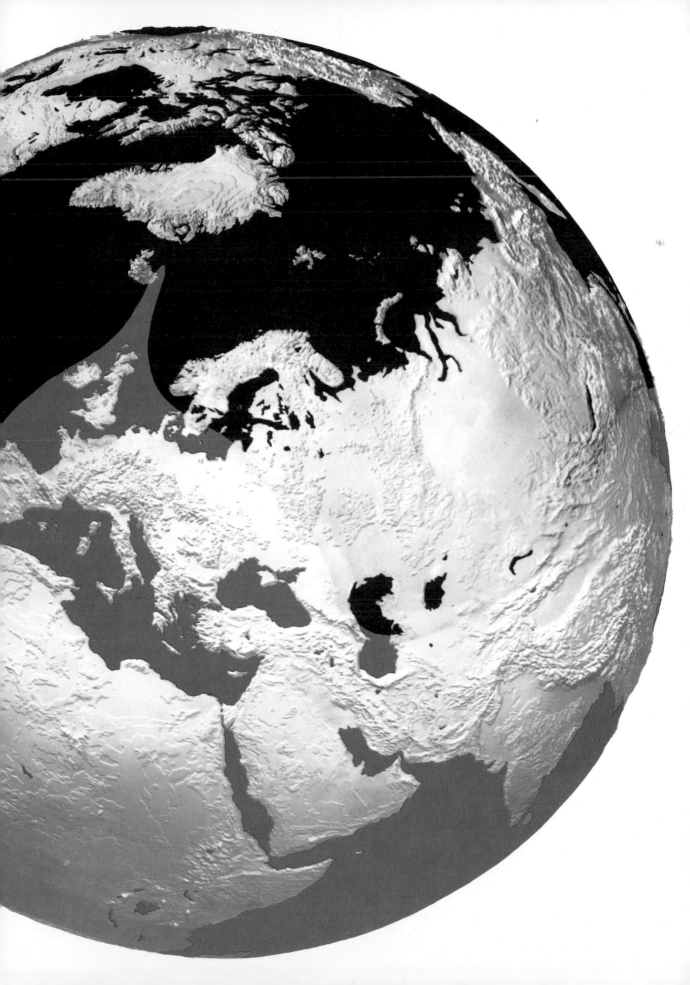

Below: a painted bas-relief from the temple at Thebes, in Egypt, showing boats being loaded for the journey to Punt. Like many accounts of early voyages, the story of the expedition to Punt is remarkably complete in some ways, but deficient in others. For example, we are never told where Punt was.

# Into the Unknown

As the high-prowed Egyptian ships sailed south down the coast of East Africa, their captains searched for signs of life. The sandy foreshore, backed by thick jungle, seemed unending. Monkeys chattered in the trees, and on moonlit nights the sailors could see the distant shadowy forms of wild animals. But there was no sign of people. Did the land of Punt really exist? How much farther must they sail before they reached that legendary country?

Many months had passed since the small fleet had left Egypt and set out down the Red Sea. To the 30 Sudanese slaves pulling on the oars of each vessel in the tropical heat, it must have seemed an unendurably long journey. And to what end? Simply to bring back a cargo of trees.

Nearly 1,500 years before the birth of Christ, Queen Hatshepsut, the powerful and beautiful ruler of Upper and Lower Egypt, had issued a decree. A temple was to be built at Thebes, on the banks of the Nile, to the glory of Amon-Re, king of the gods. Like no other temple in the land, it was to be approached by a terraced garden

Below: the temple at Thebes. Queen Hatshepsut sent her expedition to Punt for myrrh trees, unobtainable in Egypt, to plant on the temple terraces.

Above: the Egyptian explorers in procession carrying palm leaves. This is one of the bas-reliefs from the temple at Thebes, telling the story of the expedition to Punt. When Queen Hatshepsut had a record of the voyage made in her temple, she little imagined that more than 3,000 years later it would be studied by scholars trying to fit together all the details of the journey.

Right: the world's first explorers were the numerous generations of pre-historic men who migrated huge distances in search of better places to live or to escape from danger. Trudging across continents, paddling down rivers and even across seas, they moved gradually through Asia, Europe, Africa, the Americas, and even southwest into Australasia. This map shows the routes they probably followed.

Probable migration routes of the earliest p

© Geographical Projects

where the spirit of the god could walk at leisure for all eternity.

Hatshepsut ordered that the garden be planted with fragrant myrrh trees, which would provide incense for the altar of Amon-Re. But these trees did not grow in Egypt. To obtain them, it was necessary to send an expedition south down the Red Sea to the distant land of Punt. Five hundred years earlier, other Egyptian voyagers had sailed to this country. But now the route to Punt was forgotten, its exact whereabouts uncertain, and the place itself hardly believed in.

Suddenly, when the Egyptians had almost given up hope of ever reaching their goal, they caught sight of some people on the fore-shore. And in the shade of the palm trees that reached almost to the water's edge, they could see the cone-shaped huts of a small village.

The explorers dropped anchor and went ashore. The people on the shore clustered around them in amazement. "How came you to this land that people know not of?" they asked. "Did you come along the paths of heaven, or have you traversed the sea and the waters of the land of the gods? Or have you come on the beams of the sun?" This was indeed Punt. The country was no mere legend.

Now the voyagers would be able to accomplish their mission.

The Egyptian expedition was outstandingly successful. Not only did the explorers return with myrrh trees for Queen Hatshepsut, but their vessels were loaded with gold, ivory, jewels, ebony, incense, and other treasures from the land of Punt. Their momentous journey had taken the Egyptians far from their native land. In frail ships, with no charts to guide them, they had sailed through vast stretches of unfamiliar sea. And in these same ships they returned in triumph to Egypt. There, on the walls of her temple, their grateful queen recorded their achievement in pictures and inscriptions that can still be seen today.

The voyage to Punt took place nearly 3,500 years ago. But it was a comparatively recent enterprise in the long story of exploration. For thousands of years before the Egyptians put out to sea, men had been making tentative journeys into the unknown.

Far back in the remote beginnings of their existence on earth, men began to roam across the world. Seeking food and shelter, or fleeing from danger, they traveled farther and farther from their original homes. Generations of prehistoric men drifted across the great land masses through Europe, Asia, Africa, and the Americas. Trudging through trackless lands and paddling down rivers in hollowed-out logs, the men of the Stone Age were the world's

Above: a prehistoric rock painting of hunters, found in what is now Rhodesia, in Africa. Prehistoric tools and weapons, and rock paintings such as this one, have been found in various parts of the world. They are the only surviving record of the wanderings of these first explorers.

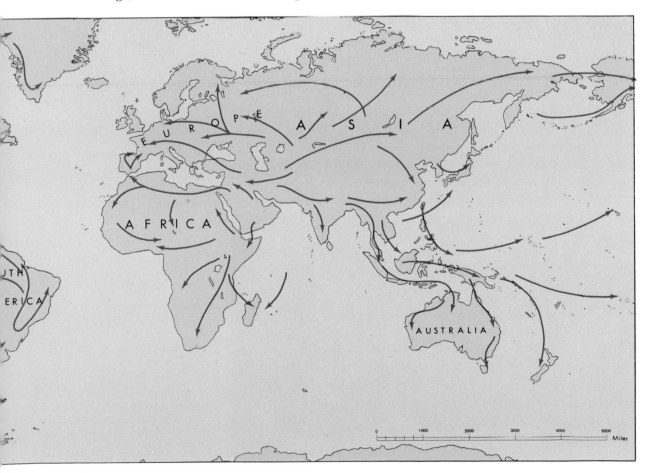

first explorers. Some of them settled where the land and climate were favorable. Others preferred the nomadic life and continued to journey on. But these men left no records of their travels. Time passed, and men began to settle in permanent communities. Then they began to explore beyond these settlements. But their ancestors' journeys had long been forgotten, and the new explorers had to learn for themselves about the lands beyond.

Defying danger, and often for scant reward, these early men left the comparative safety of their small communities and made their way into the unknown. They had no idea of the size or shape of the earth. And they lacked all but the most primitive equipment to guide them.

As soon as the early explorers put out to sea, they were at the mercy of unfamiliar currents and sudden, unpredictable squalls. Once they were out of sight of land, they were in immediate danger of being lost. By day, their course could be judged roughly in relation to the position of the sun. At night, they could navigate by the stars. But in winter the sun was often hidden by clouds, and in the dark there was the constant danger of running onto rocks. Slowly and hesitantly, these early mariners sailed and rowed their vessels into unknown seas. The shortest voyage was filled with hazard. Mariners dared not go far out of sight of land, and always carried enough food and water for the journey back to known waters. Every mile of coastline and each new island was dearly won.

Travel by land was equally hazardous. Apart from the danger of attack from wild beasts and hostile peoples, the land explorer, too, was venturing into the absolute unknown. He could carry only a limited amount of provisions, and, unless he followed a river, or established a series of water holes behind him, he ran the risk of dying from thirst. Without the example of other explorers before him, he had to decide for himself how to deal with every new situation, and every strange thing he encountered.

Many early peoples were forced to travel by need. They hoped to

Left: bell-beaker pottery of the Early Bronze Age. The bell-like shape and the method of decoration are characteristic of the work of a group of people from the Rhineland and The Netherlands, who later migrated to Britain.

find a land of plenty beyond the distant mountains, or a richer island just over the horizon. Sometimes the threat of attack by stronger neighbors forced them to flee their homes. At other times, they themselves went in search of conquest. Gradually, the growth of civilization brought another reason for travel. Man ceased to be content with bare necessities. If the materials he needed were not available near home, he set off to find them elsewhere.

The first explorers were mainly materialists, self-preservationists, aggressors, and fortune hunters. Even so, it is possible to discern another strong quality in their makeup. They possessed a streak of adventure. They could not repress a curiosity about the unknown. Behind their opportunism and varying motives lay the same rash and inexplicable desire that has inspired explorers throughout history. They wanted to be the first to set foot in new territory.

Above: some of the early rock paintings are very beautiful and full of movement. This horse comes from the famous Lascaux Cave in France, discovered in 1940. Below: a seal from around 3000 B.C., from Sumer in Mesopotamia, showing a boat with a passenger. This is one of the earliest records of boats. By this time, the Sumerians had already sailed as far as the Persian Gulf.

Above: the Nile at Aswan. The regular flooding of the river has made this valley an oasis in the surrounding sterile desert. On the fertile lands of the Nile Valley grew a civilization of great wealth and power.

Archaeological evidence provides interesting clues to the possible movements of the earliest explorers. But there are no written accounts of their travels. Only with the growth of civilization and the beginnings of written records is it possible to trace the story of the first journeys of exploration and of the men who made them.

Civilization first grew up between 5,000 and 6,000 years ago in Egypt and in Sumer. Sumer lay in southern Mesopotamia, the land between the Tigris and Euphrates rivers in what is now Iraq, eastern Syria, and southeastern Turkey. Both Egypt and Sumer depended for their livelihood on their rivers, and it was along these rivers that the people of these countries made their first voyages. In Egypt, river vessels traveled up and down the Nile, and in Mesopotamia the Sumerians navigated the Tigris and Euphrates.

The Sumerians are the first people who are known to have put out to sea for the purpose of exploration. In about 4000 B.C., Sumerian ships were sailing the waters of the Persian Gulf and had even begun to travel southward along the Asian coast to trade with India. Later, the Sumerians probably established trading contacts with Egypt.

In time, Egypt too began sending expeditions abroad. The wealth of Egypt, like that of Sumer, was mainly agricultural, and the Egyptians were forced to import many of their raw materials. One of the most important of these materials was timber, needed not only in building temples and palaces but also for constructing the ships on which Egyptian trade depended. Egypt was a land without forests. The only trees common in Egypt were palms, the wood of which is unsuitable for building seaworthy vessels. At first, the Egyptians built their boats from reeds. Later, they brought timber from the mountainous regions of the Sinai Peninsula, which lies between the two northern arms of the Red Sea. Then they discovered a source of supply in Phoenicia. This country, which corresponds approximately to the coastal areas of present-day Syria, Lebanon, and Israel, was the land of the famous cedars of Lebanon. The Egyptians soon found that these trees could provide them with an abundant source of excellent timber. So eager were the Egyptians to take advantage of this discovery that on one occasion they brought 40 shiploads of cedarwood from the Phoenician port of Byblos in a single expedition.

This voyage to Byblos, about 800 miles there and back, was made in 2600 B.C. and is the earliest recorded sea-going voyage. Many other expeditions were probably being made at this time and even before, but archaeologists have found only fragmentary evidence of them. The date at which voyaging and exploration began to take place on a significant scale may be fixed at around 2000 B.C. And in order to appreciate the achievements of those expeditions, it is important to picture the world as it appeared to the explorers of that time.

The world as it was known in 2000 B.C. was centered on the

Right: an Egyptian wall-painting of a boat of about 2000 B.C. By this time, Egyptian sailors had reached Phoenicia, and were making trading voyages to the land of Punt.

Mediterranean Sea, extending from the coastal fringes of the Middle East to the narrow Strait of Gibraltar. In this area existed the three great civilizations of Egypt, Phoenicia, and Crete. Of these, Egypt was the most powerful and influential. And it was the rise of her wealthy rulers that first stimulated trade in the Mediterranean world.

Egypt was a long, narrow country stretching south for 680 miles from the Mediterranean Sea to Aswan, just below the First Cataract (a series of rapids) on the Nile. Bounded on the east by the Red Sea, and on the west by the Libyan Desert, it drew the whole source of its life from the fertile valley of the Nile.

Mediterranean sailors entered Egypt through the marshy lagoons and sandy islands of the Nile Delta. As they sailed on up the Nile, they passed the sacred city of Heliopolis, an important religious and cultural center where work had just begun on a great temple to the sun god Re. Soon afterward, they had their first glimpse of the three pyramids at Giza (now Al Jīzah). Each nearly 500 feet high, and built from some 2 million stone blocks, the pyramids served as tombs for the kings of Egypt, and were taller than any building known to man until modern times. The largest of the three was the Great Pyramid, built in around 2600-2500 B.C. Near it stood the Sphinx. This 240-foot-long monument with the head of a king on the body of a lion was probably made in about 2600 B.C.

Twelve miles farther south was Memphis. The sailor traveling up the river reached the city just as he left the Nile Delta and set out up the mighty main stream of the river. Memphis was one of the five cities from which, at different times, the Egyptian kings ruled their land. Enclosed by a defensive wall of gleaming white limestone,

Right: the gold mask of Tutankhamon—this mask covered the face of the pharaoh's *mummy* (preserved body) in his tomb. It shows clearly the artistry of the Egyptian craftsmen.

Below: the Sphinx at Giza (Al Jīzah), with the Pyramid of Chephren behind it. These enormous stone monuments, built some 4,500 years ago, were then —and remain—wonders of the world.

it was a city of magnificent temples and fine houses.

After sailing 300 miles farther up the Nile, ships arrived at Thebes (just across the river from present-day Luxor). At that time, Thebes was an unimportant village. It was, however, destined to become the richest and most powerful city in the world. Nearby, in the barren Valley of the Kings, generations of pharaohs (rulers of Egypt after about 1370 B.C.) would be buried.

By 2000 B.C., Egypt had an estimated population of 750,000. Under King Amenemhet I, the country was entering its most prosperous period. To this Middle Kingdom (2050–1800 B.C.) belongs the finest of Egyptian craftsmanship by jewelers, carpenters, carvers, and glaziers, who worked in gold, silver, colored stones, rare woods, ivory, ebony, and glass. It was also a period when literature, art, and building flourished in the 15-mile-wide strip of land down the long course of the Nile.

About 260 miles northeast of Egypt lay the narrow strip of fertile coast occupied by the Phoenicians. Bordered by the Lebanon Mountains to the east and the Mediterranean on the west, Phoenicia

Below: the Middle East, showing the cities and empires of the ancient world. It was here, and in particular in Egypt on the banks of the Nile and in Sumer between the Tigris and the Euphrates, that civilization first grew up between 5,000 and 6,000 years ago.

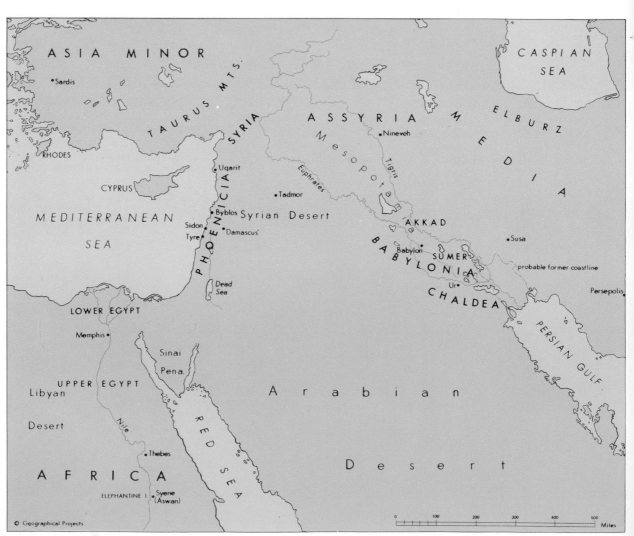

was about 200 miles long and 12 miles wide. At various times the country lay under the influence of Egypt, Babylonia, and the Hittite Empire (in what is now central Turkey), and it did not become independent until about 1100 B.C. Already in 2000 B.C., however, the Phoenicians were a formidable and enterprising people, though their civilization was very different from that of their Egyptian neighbors. They looked seaward for their livelihood, and their coastline was dotted with ports. The largest of these ports were independent city-states ruled by merchant kings. But although not formally united, the Phoenicians cooperated against common enemies. Their main activity was commerce and their greatest skill lay in sailing.

Following the Mediterranean coast to Phoenicia, Egyptian ships came first to the small coastal towns where Phoenician ships lay at anchor. When the sailors saw the snow-capped mountains of Lebanon, they knew they were approaching the important city of Tyre. Built mainly on an offshore island, and partly on the mainland, Tyre was a characteristic Phoenician port. Cities sited on rocky headlands and islands protected by chains of rocks were ideally suited to a maritime people who preferred to fight their battles on the sea. Tyre had two harbors, and the town, closely packed with houses rising to several stories, had been constructed on the rocks. Within this island fortress lived an expanding population of sailors, ship-builders, weavers, cloth dyers, and timber merchants.

Above: ruins of Tyre, the Phoenician seaport built largely on an island, and partly on the adjoining mainland. Below: a clay tablet inscribed in cuneiform (wedge-shaped) letters. The tablet is a letter from the King of Byblos to the ruler of Egypt, asking for help against invaders. Part reads, "... if no troops come, then the territory is lost." In fact, the troops did not come.

Some of Tyre's earliest inhabitants had moved to the city from the nearby port of Sidon, 25 miles farther up the coast. Together, the cities of Sidon and Tyre became famous for their cloth, which was dyed a red-purple color. They exported it to Egypt, and, later, to Greece and Rome where it was made into royal robes.

Yet another hundred miles north lay Byblos, the center of export for the cedarwood that was brought down from the forests on the slopes of the mountains of Lebanon. Byblos was an important trading center, not only for the Egyptians, but also for the peoples of Mesopotamia who traveled regularly to the land of cedars. These people were the Babylonians, descendants of a Semitic race who had conquered the inhabitants of Sumer.

The Babylonians also traded at Ugarit, possibly the most im-

portant of the Phoenician cities. The most northerly Phoenician port, Ugarit was situated opposite the eastern tip of Cyprus. In its royal palace were kept the state archives—clay tablets that recorded the extensive commercial activities of the Phoenicians. But, unlike Tyre and Sidon, the city of Ugarit fell into decay. In time, it was forgotten and only by chance rediscovered in A.D. 1927.

Like the Egyptians, the Phoenicians imported ivory, gold, and other raw materials. In their city workshops, these materials were turned into manufactured goods for export. But, unlike the Egyptians, the Phoenicians were wholesalers, retailers, and deliverers. By carrying their goods across the seas, the Phoenicians gained the experience that enabled them to become the greatest of the world's first explorers.

Above: the Octopus Vase, an elegant example of Minoan pottery. It was made in about 1500 B.C., and shows the octopus among seaweed and coral.

Left: the Throne Room at Knossos. The throne is alabaster, and stone benches are placed against the walls. The paintings of griffins in a landscape are modern reconstructions based on original fragments found in the ruins.

21

In contrast to the heavily fortified Phoenician ports, the towns of the Minoans of Crete—the third great Mediterranean civilization—were unprotected. The island of Crete provided its own defense. Four hundred miles from Egypt, 500 miles from Phoenicia, and about 80 miles from Greece, Crete was, at this time, unassailable. The Minoans also possessed a fleet quite capable of dealing with any marauders who might attempt an attack from the sea. Minoan prosperity, like that of the Phoenicians, depended on trade. During the Middle Minoan period (1900–1580 B.C.), commerce with Egypt, Italy, Spain, and the Middle East made Crete rich. Arriving at the southern port of Komo, ships from Egypt unloaded their cargoes of linen and gold destined for the palace cities of Phaestos, a few miles away, and Mallia and Knossos on the north of the island. From Komo, a well-established road led through the mountains to Knossos.

Knossos was already a busy city which, with its port, had an estimated population of 100,000. It had a royal palace with modern comforts that included bathrooms and flushing water closets. At Knossos lived the king of the region, who united with the rulers of other parts of the island to form a strong federal government. The kings controlled the agriculture, industry, and trade of Crete.

The Cretan standard of living may not have been as high as that of the Egyptians, but, nevertheless, theirs was a civilization which employed the skills of gem cutters, fresco painters, and spinners of delicate glass ornaments. The beautifully painted pottery of the Minoans was renowned. It was their chief export, and was shipped all over the Mediterranean.

Apart from the Egyptians, Phoenicians, and Minoans, no other Mediterranean people who are concerned with the story of exploration were sufficiently advanced by 2000 B.C. to be regarded as a civilization. But the early voyagers from Egypt, Phoenicia, and Crete brought their knowledge and ideas as well as their goods to other communities living around the Mediterranean at this time. And as these communities developed, they produced their own explorers.

Between 2000 B.C. and the first centuries after the birth of Christ, as one great civilization after another rose to power and then declined, the early explorers extended the frontiers of the known world. They journeyed throughout the Mediterranean and into the Atlantic Ocean. They explored the continent of Africa. They crossed the Indian Ocean, and they probed the interior of Asia. In the face of seemingly insurmountable handicaps, they accomplished amazing feats of exploration. They were the forerunners of many great discoverers of far later times, who, without knowing it, were often following the heroic pioneers, the world's first explorers.

Right: the continents of the Old World—Europe, Africa, Asia, and Australia—showing the main physical features and the chief cities of today.

# The Egyptians Explore

# 2

Foreign trade made Egypt the wealthiest country of the ancient world. A civilization of such magnificence could not have come into existence if the nation had been content to rely entirely on its own natural resources. The well-irrigated delta and valley of the Nile provided wheat to feed the people. And there was flax for linen clothing. But these were basic necessities. The standard of luxury reached by the kings and the ruling class by the time of the Old Kingdom (2700–2200 B.C.) required more exotic commodities.

Gold and silver, needed for works of art in palaces and pyramid tombs, were brought from the mines of Syria, Nubia (in present-day Sudan), and from Punt. Copper for making tools and weapons, malachite (a green mineral used for ornaments and mosaics), and turquoise came to Memphis in the saddle-packs of donkeys which followed the caravan routes across the desert from Sinai. To obtain tin, voyages were made to Spain. To provide granite for the great temples of Karnak and Thebes, there were long journeys to the quarries at the First Cataract, more than 100 miles away. Even a vital raw material such as wood had to be brought from Phoenicia.

To obtain these products, the Egyptians had to become ship-builders and sailors. Although they were never such accomplished mariners as the Phoenicians (whom they were later to employ), they learned to navigate their main highway, the Nile, in boats of their own construction. These were combined rowing and sailing ships with curved, pointed prows, designed to land on the riverbanks and to negotiate lagoons and rapids. When the Egyptians ventured into the rougher waters of the Mediterranean, and had to make their way through the coral reefs in the Red Sea, their ships were enlarged, on much the same pattern, into 70-foot-long vessels with oblong sails.

Above: a caravan of Amorite nomads, from a tomb painting of one of the later Egyptian pharaohs. The Egyptian civilization was enriched by goods brought to its cities from distant places. But only some of the luxuries the Egyptians craved could be bought from nomad merchants. For others, they had to travel themselves. Below: a wall-painting of Egyptian goldsmiths (bottom) and carpenters at work.

Above: King Pepy II, who came to the throne when only six years old, seated on his mother's lap. This statue dates from about 2230 B.C. Rulers under the Old Kingdom (2700-2200 B.C.) sent expeditions abroad for the luxuries they could not obtain at home.

For traveling overland, the Egyptians used pack donkeys and bullock carts. Camels, which are commonly associated with Egypt, were not used as carriers until about 500 B.C. Great caravans of pack animals set out regularly from Syene, the most southerly Egyptian town, on journeys into the Sudan lasting for some months. Several such expeditions were made around 2270 B.C. during the reigns of Mernere and his successor, Pepy II (who came to the throne as a child of six), by an explorer named Herkhuf, governor of Egypt's southern province. Herkhuf returned to Egypt with many of the luxuries the Egyptians longed for—ivory, ebony, frankincense, and skins. But from one expedition he brought back a special treasure—a Pygmy from one of the Sudanese tribes. The Pygmy caused a sensation in Egypt, and Herkhuf was rewarded with splendid gifts.

Herkhuf, like the other governors of southern Egypt, was concerned with defending the frontier from attack by Sudanese tribes and protecting Egypt's trading expeditions in Sudan. The governors also organized voyages to Punt, the "land of the gods" at the south of the Red Sea. This country had a legendary fascination for the Egyptians, who believed it to have been the home of their earliest ancestors. And from this land came one of the most highly sought products in all Egypt—incense. To obtain this sweet-scented substance, used in the worship of the gods, the Egyptians undertook some of their longest and most dangerous expeditions.

In about 2500 B.C., King Sahure sent ships to bring back incense from the distant land of Punt. The success of the voyage was proudly recorded. Sahure's ships returned laden, not only with incense, but with quantities of other priceless treasures from the land of the gods. Eighty thousand measures of myrrh, 6,000 weights of electrum (a gold-silver alloy), and 2,600 logs of costly wood (probably ebony) were brought from Punt to Egypt. These figures sound impressive, even though it is not known what the measures represent. The fleet also took back a number of "dwarfs" (Pygmies), who, like Herkhuf's Pygmy after them, were employed as dancers at religious festivals and court entertainments.

Egyptian ships had probably visited Punt before the time of Sahure, but his was the first expedition to have been recorded. Even so, there are no details of the port from which the fleet set out, nor of how many ships there were, nor of how far they traveled. Nor do any of the inscriptions mention where the land of Punt was situated.

For hundreds of years, scholars have tried to discover the whereabouts of this mysterious country which was of such importance to the ancient Egyptians. It now seems certain that Punt was somewhere on the Red Sea coast of Somaliland, but exactly where no one knows. Many other locations have, however, been suggested. Temple inscriptions describe Punt as lying "on both sides of the sea." This has been taken to refer to the point at which the Red Sea narrows to a 20-mile channel between the east coast of Africa and present-day Southern Yemen. Slightly farther south, the land on either side of the Gulf of Tajura near Djibouti in the French Territory of Afars and Issas also fits the description. Because some of the Egyptian expeditions to Punt brought back antimony (used in the making of rouge and for hardening copper), it has been suggested that Punt may have lain as far south as Mozambique—probably the only part of Africa where antimony could have been mined at the time of the Egyptian voyages. But, if so, the Egyptians would have had to travel 4,000 miles down the African coast to reach their destination.

During the centuries after Sahure's expedition, at least 11 further

Mentuhotep sent a trading expedition to the land of Punt.

Right: this map of ancient Egypt shows the voyage to Byblos, the great voyages down the Red Sea to Punt, and Herkhuf's journey into the Sudan.

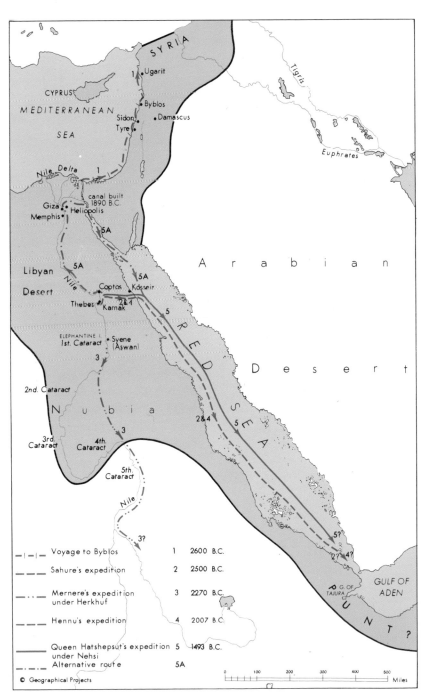

27

Above: the men of Punt bringing their myrrh trees as gifts for the Egyptians. Among all the riches that the explorers brought back from Punt, these trees were valued most highly. The incense they provided was used in ceremonies in the Egyptian temples.

voyages were made to Punt. But nearly 500 years passed before the next expedition of which we have a detailed record. This took place in 2007 B.C., when an Egyptian called Hennu was ordered to send a ship to Punt for myrrh. "I left the Nile," wrote Hennu, "with 3,000 men." Why so many? Apparently only one ship set sail down the Red Sea for Punt. The great majority of the men were probably slaves needed to carry the materials necessary for building ships across the 90 miles of desert from one of the Nile cities to the sea. Until a canal was dug between the Nile Delta and the Red Sea by Sesostris II in about 1890 B.C., this was Egypt's only way of transporting ships to its eastern seaboard. Hennu records that he sank 15 wells for drinking water on the journey, and issued each man with 2 jars of water and 20 small loaves a day during the march. Then, writes Hennu, "I reached the sea, built the ship, and sent it off."

After Hennu's expedition, the Egyptians appear to have lost interest in seafaring and travel. Concerned with their own internal prosperity, religious cults, and civilized living, they were content to let the ships and caravans of other countries carry their goods for them. But the use of these middlemen inevitably led to an increase in the cost of merchandise. This may well have been one reason for

Left: Hennu, who in 2007 B.C. took a ship to Punt for myrrh. In the 500 years before Hennu's voyage, no detailed records were kept of Egyptian journeys to Punt. Hennu, however, left details of his expedition, and of the organization of the trip.

the greatest of all the Egyptian expeditions to Punt, which was carried out by order of Queen Hatshepsut in 1493 B.C.

Queen Hatshepsut was the first woman to rule Egypt. Officially coregent, first with her husband and then with her stepson, she gradually assumed all the powers of state, and adopted the titles of ruler for herself alone. She was a gifted, ruthless, and beautiful woman. Her profile portrait, preserved among the rock carvings of her temple at Thebes, shows her with almond eyes, full lips, a finely modeled nose, and a graceful neck.

At the time of Hatshepsut's rise to power in about 1500 B.C., more than 500 years had passed since the last Egyptian voyage to Punt. The vital supplies of incense, which Egypt imported from abroad, were in greater demand than ever. One temple alone is reported to have burned over 300,000 bushels of incense on its altars in a single year. This incense was brought in heavily guarded caravans from the Hadhramaut in southern Arabia, and by the time it reached Egypt it had become extremely expensive. At the same time, the mines of Nubia, Egypt's chief source of gold, had been worked out, and the country was running short of funds with which to purchase such costly imports. Hatshepsut desperately needed to find a way of breaking the Hadhramaut's incense monopoly and of replenishing her stocks of gold.

It was probably Hatshepsut's ambitious chancellor and chief adviser, Senmut, who suggested that the queen should organize an expedition to the land of Punt. Senmut may have gained some knowledge of Hennu's expedition to Punt from inscriptions on the rocks of a tomb in the Wadi Hammamat, a stone-quarrying center to the northeast of Thebes between the Nile and the Red Sea. At all events, Senmut knew that both incense and gold were to be found in Punt and that, if Hatshepsut could succeed in repeating the journey of her forebears, it would add greatly to her prestige as queen.

Although economic necessity and personal ambition may have been the primary motives for the expedition, a less material inspiration was Hatshepsut's devotion to Egypt's state god Amon-Re. To the glory of this king of gods, Hatshepsut built a magnificent new temple at Thebes. Cut into the massive yellow cliffs on the west bank of the Nile, this temple remains today in a fair state of preservation. It is possible to visualize the great stepped terraces leading up to the temple where Queen Hatshepsut planted the myrrh trees that her sailors brought back from Punt.

As no Egyptian ships had sailed to Punt for so long, there was some doubt about the wisdom of the expedition. But the oracle of the god was consulted, and it pronounced firmly that the route was to be re-explored. Ships were prepared for the voyage and the crews were carefully chosen. The expedition was placed under the leadership of a man named Nehsi.

Left: Egyptians rowing to Punt, from the temple at Thebes. Although the ships had sails, for much of the time they relied on slaves to row them.

Right: Queen Hatshepsut in the form of a sphinx. She was a forceful, ambitious woman who came to power first as the wife of her half-brother Thutmose II. After his death, she took over his power, and her monuments show a truly regal dignity.

The carvings in Hatshepsut's temple at Thebes show five ships departing for Punt, but this may be symbolic. It seems probable that 20 or more vessels set sail for the south. Their port of departure is a matter of speculation. Like Hennu's ship, the vessels, or the materials for building them, were probably carried across the desert from Coptos (modern Kuft), on the east bank of the Nile, to the Red Sea port of Kosseir (modern Al Qusayr), about 300 miles south of Suez. But possibly Queen Hatshepsut had reopened the Nile-Red Sea canal which had been allowed to silt up since its creation by Sesostris II 400 years earlier. If so, the ships would have set out from Thebes, sailed north down the Nile to the delta, turned east into the canal, and been hauled or rowed through this man-made waterway to the head of the Gulf of Suez. Depending on the exact location of Punt, the whole voyage may have taken as little as 14 months or as long as 3 years.

On arrival, the fleet anchored offshore, and the Egyptians presented King Perehu and Queen Eti of Punt with gifts of knives, necklaces, and glass beads. During this ceremony, it is recorded, the Egyptian sailors could hardly conceal their laughter at the extraordinary appearance of Queen Eti. With her broad shoulders, stunted torso, and thick, misshapen thighs, she was unlike any woman they had ever seen.

The people of Punt prepared a banquet for Nehsi and his crew, and friendly relations were soon established between the two peoples. Then, the business of trading began. The Egyptians probably exchanged glass beads and trinkets for the incense trees and other treasures that were carefully counted out or weighed. Thirty-one saplings, each in a special wooden tub, were carried to the ships and stowed on board. Soon the Egyptian vessels were "very heavy with marvels of the land of Punt; all goodly fragrant woods of God's Land, heaps of incense-resin, fresh incense trees, ebony and pure ivory, gold . . . cinnamon wood, eye cosmetic, baboons, monkeys, dogs, skins of the southern panther. . . ." The Egyptians also took with them some of the people of Punt, "natives and their children,"

Above: a model of an Egyptian sea-going ship. Originally, the Egyptians built their ships from reeds because there was little wood in Egypt. But reed boats were often unseaworthy, and the Egyptians began to use wood from the Sinai Peninsula. Later, they imported Phoenician cedarwood.

Below left: the Egyptian party giving the gifts they had brought with them to King Perehu and Queen Eti of Punt.

together with portraits of Punt's rulers, King Perehu and Queen Eti.

The return of Nehsi and his crew to Egypt was greeted with a wave of popular enthusiasm. A public holiday was proclaimed and the explorers marched through the streets in procession, carrying the treasures of the land of Punt for all to see. There were speeches, banquets, and religious celebrations. The mariners were given a royal reception in Queen Hatshepsut's palace, where Hatshepsut sat on her throne with Nehsi and Senmut at her feet. All around her lay piles of exotic goods, incense, and precious metals. "Such a treasure," the temple inscription ends, "was never brought for any king who has ruled since the beginning."

No other Egyptian expedition was on a comparable scale. After Queen Hatshepsut's death in 1482 B.C., her stepson and successor Thutmose III engaged in a series of military campaigns to expand the Egyptian Empire. Under his leadership, Egyptian armies pushed north and east through Palestine and Syria. When they reached the Euphrates River, it is recorded, elephant hunts were organized in which as many as 120 animals were killed for their tusks. On this occasion, Thutmose, who had come unscathed through all his military adventures, narrowly escaped death when a huge elephant charged him.

During his reign, which lasted until about 1436 B.C., Thutmose commissioned the Minoans of Crete to do much of the fetching and

Below: a procession of Egyptians carrying palms, from the records of the expedition at Thebes.

Above: Thutmose III (right), the stepson and successor of Hatshepsut. This portrait is on a colonnade at Thebes. Thutmose spent much of his reign fighting in Palestine and Syria, and under him the Egyptian Empire reached its greatest size.

carrying of Egyptian trading goods. At that time, the Minoans were masters of the Mediterranean, and their ships were to be seen in every port from Byblos to the shores of southern Spain. But the power and civilization of Crete came to a sudden and dramatic end soon after it had reached its greatest heights. In about 1400 B.C., Crete lay in ruins. Possibly an earthquake destroyed the island, but it may have fallen before invading forces from the city of Mycenae in southern Greece.

Five hundred years later, Egypt, torn by internal strife and weakened by foreign invaders, had also lost much of its former greatness. This decline in Egypt's power was recorded in the travel diary of Wen-Amun, an envoy sent to the Phoenicians in 1080 B.C.

The Egyptians were going to Phoenicia for cedarwood as they had done ever since that first recorded expedition in 2600 B.C. Wen-Amun had been commissioned to obtain the wood for the temple of Amon-Re at Thebes. But the high priest of the temple had supplied him with only limited goods for exchange, and Egypt no longer possessed the prestige to compensate for this lack of funds.

Wen-Amun was treated badly. He was robbed and insulted. "The prince of Byblos sent to tell me, 'Get out of my harbor,' " he wrote. For 19 days Wen-Amun was kept waiting before being summoned to see the prince, who asked him haughtily, "What kind of beggar's journey is this that you have been sent on?"

Vainly did Wen-Amun remind the prince of happy historical precedents. It had no effect until a messenger who had been sent back to Egypt returned with sufficient goods to exchange for the cedars. Even then, Wen-Amun was harried during the loading of the timber, and, as a final insult, the prince told him: "See that you get on your way, and do not make the bad time of the year an excuse for remaining here."

The star of Egypt was in decline. Rising now to dominate the whole scene of exploration were the Phoenicians. These daring and accomplished sailors embarked on more distant and ambitious voyages than any undertaken by the mariners of Egypt. The Phoenicians made themselves the masters of the Mediterranean Sea and became the first explorers to venture through the Strait of Gibraltar into the vast and unknown waters of the Atlantic Ocean.

Above: a pendant from Byblos, inlaid with semiprecious stones. Dating from about 2000 B.C., this pendant was probably made by a local artist, influenced by Egyptian craftsmen.

Left: an Egyptian wall-painting of two figures, identified as Minoans, carrying ingots. Thutmose III hired the Minoans of Crete to do much of the transportation of Egyptian goods.

35

Below: Phoenician *hippoi*—river craft —shown on a wall relief in a palace at Khorsabad, Iraq. The Phoenician boats, which are manned by oarsmen are carrying cedar logs for trading.

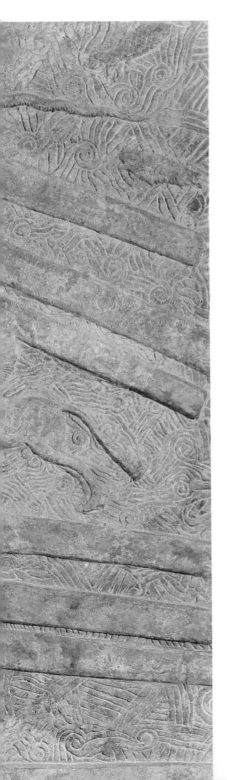

# Phoenician Pioneers

# 3

About 600 years before the birth of Christ, a fleet of vessels set out on an extraordinary 23,000-mile journey into the unknown. Manned by Phoenician sailors, these ships were embarking on one of the greatest voyages in the history of exploration—the first circumnavigation of Africa.

This was a voyage so extraordinary for its time that many people doubt whether it could ever have taken place. There is evidence that the Phoenicians were making trading voyages as early as 2700 B.C. Their prowess as sailors is recorded in the Old Testament and in classical writings. From tools, weapons, and other such remains discovered in various places, archaeologists have been able to plot the extent of many of the Phoenician voyages. But no trace has ever been found of their feat of circumnavigation. Is it possible that the Phoenicians could have made such a journey over 2,000 years before the generally accepted first rounding of the African continent by the Portuguese? And what kind of people were the Phoenician explorers who might have undertaken such a daring expedition?

Above: an old map showing Phoenicia, on the eastern coast of the Mediterranean.

Above: Phoenician pendants, glass beads in the shape of heads, modeled on a sand core in Carthage before 300 B.C. The Phoenicians established their colonies all around the Mediterranean.

Below: a goddess carved in ivory, from what is now Syria. It shows the influence of similar figures from the Aegean area, particularly in the flounced skirt and bare chest, and demonstrates the Phoenician aware-ness of the world in which they traded.

The Phoenicians were the Canaanites of the Old Testament. They were a Semitic race, believed to have originated in the Persian Gulf area. In about 3000 B.C., they settled in the land between the mountains of Lebanon and the Mediterranean Sea. There they founded the cities of Sidon and Tyre, probably naming Tyre after their original home on the island of Tyros (modern Bahrain in the Persian Gulf). Their 200-mile coastline was fertile but they were prevented from expanding eastward by hostile neighbors. As the Phoenician population grew, their small country became over-crowded. It was logical that when this happened they should turn increasingly to the sea for their living.

Ideally situated for trade halfway between two prosperous nations—Egypt and the land of the Hittites—the Phoenicians began to make their living by fetching and carrying merchandise by both land and sea. Phoenicia was on the main caravan routes between northern Africa and the Mesopotamian countries, and the Phoenicians carried goods overland as far as Babylon. As the earliest traders to operate according to an organized plan, they spread out farther and farther from their great seaports, founding small colonies all over the Mediterranean. Phoenician colonies grew up in Sicily and Cyprus, and as far west as Cádiz in southern Spain. They even had a small trading post at Memphis in the commercial heart of Egypt.

The Phoenicians combined their abilities as traders with other skills. They were miners, metallurgists, shipbuilders, and dyers. The cedar forests of Lebanon gave them timber which they sold abroad, and another valuable export was the transparent glass that they made from the white sand of their seashore. The alphabet which they invented around 1000 B.C. formed the basis of the Greek alphabet, on which were later founded the Roman and all western alphabets.

The Phoenicians' fame as dyers probably gave rise to their name. *Phoenician* comes from a Greek word meaning *red-purple,* an allusion to the special dye that they used. The dye came from a shellfish found on the Syrian shore that gave off a defensive juice called *purpura.* Cloth dyed in this juice was in great demand all over the East, where the color became a mark of rank and dignity.

It might have been hoped that so versatile a race, and the inventors of the alphabet, would have left records of their early exploration. But the Phoenicians appear to have been deliberately secretive, keeping all knowledge of their sea routes and discoveries to themselves. If they wrote down their achievements, nothing has survived. In later centuries, they even went so far as to wreck one of their own ships rather than give away its destination to a Roman competitor.

Because of this mystery about their voyages, stories of the Phoenicians' achievements are not as widely believed today as once they were. And the theory that for hundreds of years the Phoenicians held absolute trade monopolies all over the Mediterranean has also encountered some opposition. Archaeological findings indicate that

the Minoans rather than the Phoenicians must be given greater credit for pioneering voyages in the Mediterranean. But with the decline of Crete in about 1400 B.C., the Phoenician ascendancy began, and the Phoenicians have a strong claim to being the first people to have explored the whole Mediterranean from one end to the other.

Historians believe that Phoenician sailors were the first to learn how to navigate by the Pole Star. Their maritime accomplishments were so widely recognized in ancient times that other nations often found it more profitable to employ Phoenician sailors as carriers than to build their own fleets.

In about 950 B.C., the Phoenicians supplied ships and sailors for a great expedition ordered by King Solomon of Israel. Their voyage is recorded in the Old Testament: "And King Solomon made a navy of ships in Ezion-Geber [Elat, at the head of the Gulf of Aqaba] on the shore of the Red Sea. . . . And Hiram [king of Tyre in Phoenicia] sent in the navy his servants, shipmen that had knowledge of the sea, with the servants of Solomon. And they came to Ophir, and fetched from thence gold, four hundred and twenty talents, and brought it to King Solomon. . . ." The Old Testament also mentions the bringing back of "gold and silver, ivory and apes and peacocks" from Ophir.

Ophir was famous for its fine gold, and it could possibly have been the same land of Punt to which the Egyptians had traveled. Solomon's fleet may have ventured far beyond the Red Sea, for the

Above: the coastline of the Gulf of Aqaba in what is now Israel. It was from Elat, at the head of the gulf, that King Solomon's ships set forth for the land of Ophir. The castle shown here was built during the Crusades.

Right: a kneeling bronze figure of King Necho. According to Herodotus, he sponsored an expedition which sailed around the continent of Africa.

Below: the servants of Hiram of Tyre with King Solomon, from the Great Bible of King Henry VIII of England. Hiram and Solomon sent a fleet to the land of Ophir—probably in southern Arabia—to bring back gold and other precious goods.

voyage is said to have taken three years. The peacocks that they brought back could have come only from India or Ceylon, and it is possible that the fleet reached the shores of India. It seems probable, however, that Ophir lay in southern Arabia, a region that had grown immensely wealthy on the proceeds of the incense trade and where Indian merchants also came to exchange their wares.

The Phoenicians played a major part in the voyage to Ophir. Solomon's people did not care for the sea and had little experience of sailing. When they tried, on another occasion, to make a voyage to Ophir on their own, their ships are said to have fallen apart soon after being launched. The success of such an expedition depended on the shipbuilding and navigational skills of the Phoenicians. If the Phoenicians did indeed make a voyage around the African continent in about 600 B.C., those skills would have been tested to the utmost.

It is said that the Phoenician voyage around Africa was commissioned by King Necho of Egypt, who wanted to find out if he could establish a sea route from the Red Sea to the Mediterranean. At that time, no one had the faintest idea of the extent of the African continent. If King Necho did indeed sponsor such a voyage, he must have believed that if ships sailed beyond Punt, they would soon circle around the southern land mass, and so find themselves at the western end of the Mediterranean. In any case, neither he nor the sailors could have had any conception that this would mean a journey of about 23,000 miles.

The only record of this fantastic exploit is this short account by the Greek historian Herodotus, who was writing 150 years after the event:

"As for Libya [Africa], we know that it is washed on all sides by the sea except where it joins Asia, as was first demonstrated, so far as our knowledge goes, by Necho, the Egyptian king, who, after calling off the construction of the canal between the Nile and the Arabian Gulf, sent out a fleet manned by a Phoenician crew with orders to sail west-about and return to Egypt and the Mediterranean by way of the Strait of Gibraltar. The Phoenicians sailed from the Arabian Gulf into the southern ocean, and every autumn put in at some convenient spot on the Libyan coast, sowed a patch of ground,

Right: a Phoenician silver bowl. The interior is decorated with gilt, while the friezes around the outside show scenes of combat between warriors and lions, sphinxes, and winged griffins (fabulous animals, part lion, and part eagle). At various times, Phoenicia lay within the empires of Egypt and Babylonia, and the Phoenician culture bears strong traces of their influence.

ΗΡΟΔΟΤΟΣ

Left: Herodotus, the great Greek historian and traveler, who came to be known as "The Father of History." His is the only account of the Phoenician voyage around Africa, and many scholars doubt the truth of his report. One point in Herodotus' story indicates that such a voyage had taken place—but this point Herodotus himself did not believe. He records that the sailors reported that when they sailed west around the south of Africa, the sun was on their right—that is, to the north. When sailing west in the Southern Hemisphere, the sun does appear on the right at noon.

and waited for next year's harvest. Then, having got in their grain, they put to sea again, and after two full years rounded the Pillars of Hercules [Strait of Gibraltar] in the course of the third, and returned to Egypt. These men made a statement which I do not myself believe, though others may, to the effect that as they sailed on a westerly course round the southern end of Libya, they had the sun on their right—to northward of them. This is how Libya was first discovered to be surrounded by sea. . . ."

Tantalizingly inadequate though it is, Herodotus' account has become a central part of the belief that the Phoenicians are among the greatest sailors in history. For, if this voyage did take place, it must rank as one of the most amazing feats of seamanship ever accomplished.

Herodotus himself apparently accepted the circumnavigation as a fact, except for the Phoenicians' story about the position of the sun. Yet, if anything, this is the most authentic detail of the account. For ships sailing in a westerly direction in the Southern Hemisphere would indeed find that, at noon, the sun was on their right, that is, to the north of them. The very remark which made Herodotus' report seem incredible in his own time indicates that daring sailors did make a successful voyage around the African continent at a very early date.

There have been many attempts to amplify Herodotus' brief statement and to reconstruct the details of the Phoenician voyage. Those who believe that the voyage really took place point out that King Necho had a good reason for promoting it. He was eager to stimulate Egyptian trade and had been trying to reopen the ancient canal between the Red Sea and the Nile which had fallen into disuse over the centuries. But this work was halted when Necho was warned by an oracle that the canal would help enemies to invade his country. He was therefore anxious to know if there was any route other than the Nile canal by which ships could get from the Red Sea into the Mediterranean. He was curious to discover how long it would take to travel by such a route, and to find out what trading possibilities existed beyond Punt. An added incentive for such a voyage was the report that gold was to be found in what is now Rhodesia.

It is interesting to see just how the Phoenicians could have carried out this long and hazardous voyage. They would probably have

Above: coral islands in the Red Sea off the coast of Ethiopia. By 600 B.C., the canal between the Red Sea and the Nile had fallen into disuse. Necho may have ordered a voyage around Africa to find a new way from the Red Sea to the Mediterranean Sea.

made the voyage in the same large compact vessels, with a high convex prow and stern, that they used for trading voyages. These ships may have been as much as 130 feet long and 33 feet across. They had covered decks and a single large sail. They were manned by 30 to 50 oarsmen. In addition, they must have carried a few replacements in case of illness or death, and possibly a certain number of soldiers, together with a group of officers under the captain.

With their fragile ships, and primitive equipment, the Phoenicians would have seized gratefully on the natural advantages of wind or current to help them on their way. Any reconstruction of their voyage can therefore best be based on just those same natural conditions. The expedition would have set out from the Gulf of Aqaba, probably in late November. The ships must have been fully equipped for a long voyage and, according to Herodotus, they carried a fast-growing wheat which could be planted and reaped for food during the journey.

The autumn start meant that the northeast monsoon was against the Phoenician sailors, and they would have had to row until they were out of the Red Sea. But, when they had rounded Cape Guardafui on the northeastern tip of Somaliland, the same monsoon would have helped them down the coast of Somaliland as far as the equator. In spring, they could take advantage of the southeast trade wind to reach the Mozambique Channel between mainland Mozambique and the Malagasy Republic. Once the ships were in this channel, the swift-

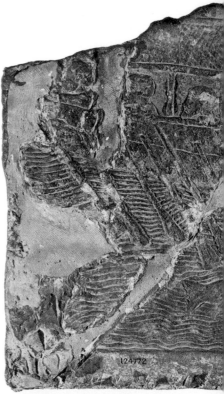

Left: the African continent, showing the probable route of the Phoenicians on their 23,000-mile expedition around Africa, 600 years before the birth of Christ. The map also shows the main currents which would have helped or hindered the Phoenicians on such a long and perilous voyage.

flowing South Equatorial Current would have borne them south-ward, and the Agulhas Current helped to carry them around the southern tip of Africa.

At this point in their voyage, the Phoenicians would have entered dangerous waters. The passage around the Cape of Good Hope is a treacherous one, where sudden squalls are frequent and the belt of westerly winds now known as the "roaring forties" can sweep vessels far out to sea. The Phoenicians must have edged their way slowly along 1,000 miles of coastline between what are now Port Elizabeth and Cape Town.

As they rounded Cape Agulhas, they would have found that at last the coastline was running northward. In May or June, they may have landed, probably about 150 miles up the west coast of Africa in

Above: a Phoenician galley, of the kind used for long voyages. It has two banks of oars with a deck above, and along the deck are hung the warriors' shields. Although such ships had a single sail, they were often rowed. Necho's men would have used ships like this.

St. Helena Bay. There, they would have sown their first crop of wheat, repaired their vessels, and rested while they waited for the wheat to ripen. In the subtropical climate of southern Africa, seed sown in early June would have been ready for reaping by November. With fresh grain in their holds, the ships would have started northward in December. They would now have been away from Egypt for over a year.

With the aid of a favorable south wind and the Benguela Current, the Phoenician ships could have made steady progress up the West African coast. But soon they would have faced another hazard—lack

Below: reaping wheat, shown in an Egyptian painting on papyrus. According to Herodotus, Necho's expedition took a fast-growing wheat which the men planted and harvested during the voyage.

of water. Along the coast of South West Africa lies the Namib Desert—1,000 miles of desolate shore which receives less than an inch of rainfall a year. Because of the threat of death from thirst, the Phoenicians must have left this part of the coast behind them as quickly as possible.

With wind and current still in their favor, they would probably have reached the Bight of Biafra, off present-day Nigeria and Cameroon, in mid-March of the second year. But, as the explorers advanced into the Gulf of Guinea, they would have met with a combination of contrary winds and currents, interspersed with unexpected calms. For 2,000 miles, they must have battled against these grueling adversities, pulling hard on their long oars in the heat of the tropical sun. As the weeks and months went by, their voyage must have seemed endless. It was probably late June by the time they rounded Cape Palmas in what is now Liberia, only to find that now the Canary Current was against them.

The Phoenicians may have made their second long stop on the coast of Senegal, or continued as far as the Atlantic coast of Morocco, where they could have sown their wheat in December and reaped it the following June. From there, it was a relatively short haul up the Moroccan coast and through the Strait of Gibraltar. Once in the Mediterranean, the Phoenicians would have been in familiar waters.

Above: sunset at Lanzarote looking toward the island of Fuerteventura in the Canaries. Necho's expedition would have sailed near here on their way to the Strait of Gibraltar.

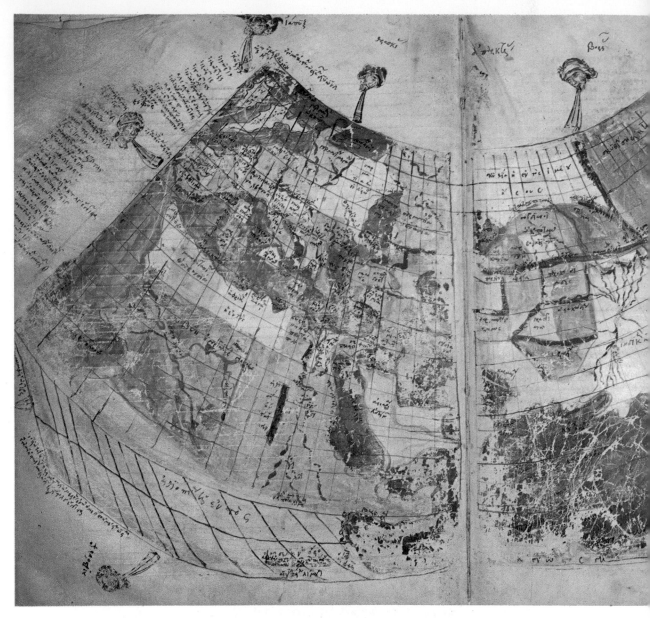

Above: a map of the world drawn in the 1200's. This map is based on the writings of the Greek geographer Ptolemy, who summed up what the ancient world knew about geography. The map pictures Africa as part of a great southern land mass, which seems to indicate either that Ptolemy knew nothing about the Phoenician expedition, or that he did not believe Herodotus' account.

The terrible uncertainties and sufferings of their long voyage were over. Neutral winds, generally favorable currents, and the sailors' own enthusiastic efforts on the home stretch would have carried the fleet safely along the north coast of Africa to the mouth of the Nile, and Egypt.

On their journey around the African continent, the Phoenicians would have had to follow every indentation of the 22,921-mile-long coastline, except in the familiar Red Sea and Mediterranean. They probably completed their journey in about three years, which (if two six-month harvesting periods are deducted) works out at a reasonable daily average of about 30 miles.

There was probably no great celebration for the returning heroes. They had brought no gold or treasure back, and their momentous

Right: a painted Egyptian pot showing giraffes. It is upon remains such as this that scholars must base their theories about ancient times. For example, this vase can be taken to prove that the Egyptians had penetrated deep into Africa, for giraffes only live south of the Sahara.

voyage had only served to prove that the route around Africa was far too long and dangerous to be considered for trading purposes. As they told the story of their voyage, one of the main points of discussion must have been the size of the African continent.

Why did Herodotus not mention this in his account? He believed, like others of his time, that the east coast of Africa turned west not far below the Gulf of Aden. The great southward extension of Africa would therefore have been one of the expedition's most remarkable discoveries. There are other questions that provide evidence for those who doubt the reality of the Phoenician voyage. Why did Herodotus fail to name the leader of the expedition? Why does he give no details of the lands that the explorers visited, or the wild beasts and the men that they must have encountered? Why are there no parallel accounts of the voyage? Later historians— Greek, Arabian, or Roman—do not confirm it. Was such a voyage remotely feasible in such early ships and without a compass? Would the Phoenicians have embarked on a long voyage in an area where they knew nothing of the prevailing winds and currents?

The most likely explanation of why Herodotus, normally an excellent reporter, was brief in his account is that his information was based on hearsay. It is possible that King Necho died before his expedition got back, and because the voyage had achieved none of its commercial aims, his successor failed to keep an official record of it. But it is equally possible that the whole incident was a fiction— a traveler's tale exaggerated over the decades. Even thorough sifting of the evidence leaves the verdict open. The Phoenician circumnavigation of Africa remains the greatest unsolved mystery in the history of exploration.

# West from Carthage

# 4

With their eyes ever looking out to sea, the Phoenicians were ill prepared to defend themselves against attack from the rear. Their cities, built on islands off the coast or on inaccessible headlands, gave them some protection from invaders. But as a people they were not unified nor collectively strong, and they eventually fell victim to the powerful armies of their Mesopotamian neighbors. When the Assyrians from the northern part of Mesopotamia swept down on Phoenicia in the 800's B.C., the Phoenician city-states withstood long sieges, but could not hold out indefinitely.

Tyre resisted longest, but in 668 B.C., even this island fortress was forced to capitulate to King Ashurbanipal of Assyria after a nine-year siege. Just under 100 years later, this "crowning city whose merchants are princes," as it is described in the Old Testament, was conquered again, this time by King Nebuchadnezzar II of Babylonia. This defeat, which was achieved after a siege of 13 years, brought the whole of Phoenicia under Babylonian rule.

The time had come for the Phoenicians to find a new home. Moreover, now that the whole Mediterranean had been opened up, a site farther west would be better placed geographically than Phoenicia as a trading center. They chose a small port on the north coast of Africa in what is now Tunisia, where there had been Phoenician settlers for some 200 years. They developed it into their new city-state of Carthage.

To the Phoenicians, Carthage seemed an ideal spot for their new capital. Like Tyre, it was well situated for defense. It was built on a triangular peninsula joined to the mainland by a narrow strip of land, and was backed by the Lake of Tunis. Besides, according to Phoenician legend, Carthage had a royal history. Dido, a princess of Tyre, was said to have fled there with some of her people. Grand-niece of the notorious Jezebel of the Bible, Dido was a fugitive not from the Assyrians, but from her tyrannical brother, King Pygmalion. She sailed first to Cyprus, and then along the desert shores of Libya to the Tunisian headland nearest Sicily.

Above left: an artist's reconstruction of Carthage as the city would have appeared at the height of its power. Notice particularly the inner harbor, with its circular enclosing wall.
Left: the ruins of Carthage today, with the sea in the distance.

Above: Ashurbanipal, the Assyrian king who captured Tyre after a nine-year siege, shown taking part in a lion hunt. He was the last great king of Assyria.

Right: a mosaic from Carthage, showing the earth goddess of the city. After the fall of Phoenicia in the 500's B.C., Carthage became the center of the Phoenician world. It grew into a capital whose riches and luxury were a legend in ancient times.

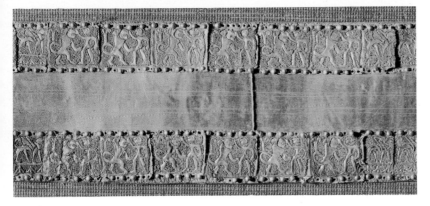

There, according to colorful legend, Dido asked Iarbas, the local king, for land on which to settle, and he derisively agreed to let her have as much as she could cover with an oxhide. But he was no match for a Phoenician. Dido cut up the hide into thin strips, and with these was able to encircle all the land she needed for a fortress. Her city was called *Kart-hadasht*—Carthage—meaning *New Capital* or *New City*.

The earliest archaeological remains found at Carthage date from about 750 B.C., although according to tradition it was founded in 814 B.C. Little is, however, known about the city until it was chosen as the new Phoenician capital. Within 300 years, Carthage had become a capital far greater than Tyre or Byblos, a city of gleaming white buildings and rich palaces overlooked by a marble temple. At the height of its power, the main city covered 30 square miles. About 70,000 people lived within a surrounding wall, some 40 feet high and 18 miles long. Determined never to suffer the fate of Tyre, Carthage maintained a garrison of 20,000 infantrymen and 4,000 cavalry. In its stables stamped and trumpeted 300 elephants of war—like those which Hannibal was later to make the most famous in history.

The most impressive feature of Carthage was its harbor. Divided into an inner and an outer section, this was a remarkable piece of maritime architecture. The inner harbor was circular, and built around a small central island. It was about 1,000 feet in diameter, and there was docking space for 200 ships. On the island was the naval headquarters, a tall building commanding a view of the sea. The harbor entrance, about 70 feet wide, could be closed against a marauding enemy by chains, and the whole harbor was surrounded by a wall so that it was possible to keep secret the number of vessels at anchor.

Out of this harbor sailed the Carthaginian warships. They patrolled the narrowest neck of water in the Mediterranean—the 100-mile wide Strait of Sicily—and so controlled all seaborne trade between east and west. From Carthage, their long ships set out for even more distant horizons. From about 550 B.C., their attention was fixed on the "outer sea" beyond the Strait of Gibraltar. The Atlantic offered them new trade routes and fresh sources of wealth.

The West African coast awaited development. From a new found port in Spain they explored farther west and discovered Madeira, the Canary Islands, and the Azores.

Carthaginian ruthlessness in trade can be seen in the way they dealt with the Tartessians, a wealthy seagoing people who occupied a large area of southern Spain. These people knew one of the greatest secrets of the "outer sea"—the way to the Tin Islands. These islands were a source of mineral wealth lying somewhere in northern waters as yet unknown to the Carthaginians. The Phoenicians were at first content to act as carriers, taking silver and tin from Tartessus across to the eastern end of the Mediterranean. But after 500 B.C., no more is heard of the Tartessians. It is thought that the Carthaginians destroyed them and seized their trade.

To develop this trade for themselves, the Carthaginians needed a good port on the Atlantic seaboard. They decided on Gades (modern Cádiz), where there had been a small Phoenician settlement since about 1100 B.C. Gades lay off the southwest coast of Spain in a typically strategic position at the end of a long island, which today

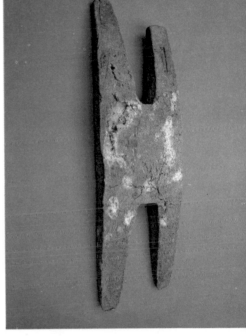

Above: one of the H-shaped ingots of Cornish tin which were exported to the Mediterranean area. Tin was a very valuable commodity, needed to mix with copper to produce bronze.

Below: a Phoenician round ship, of the type used for trading voyages. It was smaller than the galley, but, like galleys, had two banks of oars.

is attached to the Spanish mainland by a narrow arm of land.

It was from Gades that a Carthaginian navigator named Himilco set out in about 450 B.C. on the first recorded voyage into the North Atlantic. According to the Roman historian Pliny, Himilco's orders were "to explore the utmost bounds of Europe," a brief which undoubtedly included a search for the Tin Islands. Although some tin was mined in Spain, the supply was inadequate for the growing needs of the Mediterranean peoples, who needed it as an ingredient of bronze. Bronze—a mixture of nine parts of copper to one part of tin—was vital for making strong, durable weapons and tools as well as utensils and ornaments.

Himilco's voyage lasted for four months, but the records of his achievements are sparse. His expedition is referred to in Pliny's *Natural History*, which was published in A.D. 77, and in a poem called *Ora Maritima*, which was based on a Greek legend and was written by the Roman poet Avienus in the A.D. 300's. It seems likely that Himilco followed a route given to the Carthaginians under duress by the defeated Tartessians. This route is thought to have

Above: the Mediterranean world between 2000 B.C. and 140 B.C. This map shows
the civilizations which, in succession, dominated the area, controlling trade
and initiating exploration. Earliest of these civilizations were those of Egypt,
Crete, and Phoenicia. At first the Minoans of Crete held power in the Medi-

terranean but, after about 1400 B.C., the Phoenicians succeeded them. The Greeks and the Carthaginians—last of the great Mediterranean powers before the rise of the Roman Empire—existed alongside one another. The Greeks were mainly active in the eastern Mediterranean, while Carthage controlled trade in the west.

taken him up the Atlantic coast of Spain in search of the northern lands from which the Tartessians obtained their supplies of tin.

At the start of the voyage, Himilco encountered calms, shallows, and seaweed, which entangled oars and keels, and slowed down his ships. This has been interpreted as meaning that he went as far southwest as the Sargasso Sea, a large tract of water in the North Atlantic, about 2,000 miles west of the Canary Islands, notorious for its abundance of thick seaweed. But it seems unlikely that Himilco could have been driven so far off his course, and he may have been referring to the large quantities of seaweed that still collect in high summer off Cape St. Vincent, at the southwest corner of present-day Portugal.

Himilco probably followed the Spanish and French coastlines until he reached the shores of Brittany, which were mainly uninhabited. Then he may have struck northwestward across the English Channel and reached the Scilly Islands, off Cornwall in southwest England. Were these the mysterious Tin Islands? The Scilly Islands themselves may not have produced a great deal of tin, but they could have served as a depot to which tin from Cornwall was brought and then re-exported. The most controversial speculation of all is that Himilco actually reached Britain, and mistook the Cornish peninsula at Land's End for the tip of a group of islands. The rich deposits of tin found near the surface of the ground and in streams could easily have led him to think that he had discovered the so-called Tin Islands. If this did happen, it would make him the instigator of the subsequent Cornish-Mediterranean tin trade.

Unfortunately, the whole question of whether the Phoenicians or Carthaginians ever reached Cornwall remains tantalizingly unanswered. There is evidence, however, that Cornish tin did reach the Mediterranean by two different routes. It was smelted into H-shaped ingots and taken by wagon to the Island of Ictis (St. Michael's Mount, a small island off the Cornish coast which can be reached by a causeway at low tide). There, it was loaded into traders' ships. These ships may have carried the tin all the way to the Mediterranean. Alternatively, they may have unloaded the ingots on the coast of France for overland transportation to Marseille and thence by ship to the East. There are records of this route being used by 300 B.C., but it may well have existed for hundreds of years before that time.

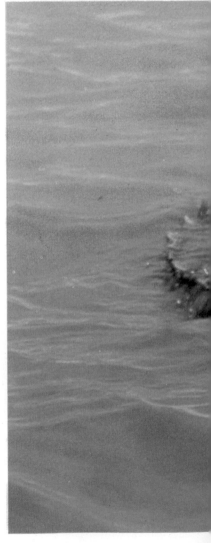

Another Carthaginian sailor has left a far more detailed account of a voyage that he made down the western coast of Africa. His name was Hanno, and he may have been the king of Carthage. The purpose of his expedition was to set up a number of Carthaginian colonies on the African coast beyond the Strait of Gibraltar. Possibly these colonies were intended to safeguard the approaches to Madeira and the Canary Islands, where the Carthaginians had discovered an important new source of raw material for the dye trade. The colonies could also be of assistance to Carthaginian ships sailing in that part of the Atlantic, and the settlers would be able to search as well for

new sources of gold and precious metals in the African interior.

Hanno set out from Carthage with 60 ships in about 450 B.C. Each ship was large enough to carry 500 immigrants and all their provisions, and was rowed by 50 oarsmen. Hanno's account of this extraordinary voyage of 30,000 settlers was recorded on a bronze tablet which was set up to commemorate the event in the temple of Saturn (Baal Hammon) in Carthage.

Having sailed through the Strait of Gibraltar, and around Tangier, Hanno's ships made their way down the Moroccan coast. A landing was made at Thymiaterium (modern Mehedia, 70 miles north of Casablanca), and the first colony was founded there. Six more towns, including one on the site of modern Essaouira and another on that

Left: some of the excavations at Mogador (present-day Essaouira) on the coast of Morocco. On his voyage down the coast of Africa, Hanno founded seven colonies on the Moroccan coast, one of them at Mogador.

Below: during their voyage, Hanno and his men sailed up a big river, where they found crocodiles and hippopotamuses. The river is now thought to have been the Senegal, because both animals are found there.

Left: Mount Cameroon. It has been suggested that this volcano is the "Chariot of the Gods" mentioned by Hanno, who might have seen the volcano erupting. But some scholars believe that Hanno did not sail so far south, and that what he saw was Mount Kakulima, on the Guinea-Sierra Leone border, with its slopes ablaze.

Above: a decorated ostrich egg bowl. Such bowls were apparently one of the most popular of Phoenician trading goods, as similar ones have been found on the sites of nearly all the known Phoenician settlements.

of Agadir, were set up about 300 miles farther south in the coastal strip at the foot of the Grand Atlas mountains.

Near the southern border of Morocco, the Carthaginian explorers made friends with the nomadic people who pastured their flocks on the banks of what was probably the Draâ River, and they stayed there for some time. Then, taking some of the nomads as interpreters, they continued south along the coast of Spanish Sahara until they came to a small offshore island at the top of a gulf. This island, which Hanno called Cerne, has been variously identified as Herne Island off Spanish Sahara, Arguin Island about 50 miles below Cape Blanc off Mauritania, or one of the small islands near the mouth of the Senegal River. Perhaps attracted to the island because it resembled the classic Phoenician defensive sites, Hanno landed all the remaining settlers there to establish what was to be the most important West African trading colony for the next 400 years.

His mission accomplished, Hanno might well have turned back, but the true spirit of exploration made him continue the voyage. Having reached the mouth of a big river which interested him, he decided to sail inland. He went up the river until he came to some high mountains which, he says, "were inhabited by forest dwellers who were attired in the skins of animals and who sought to stop us from landing by hurling stones at us." The sailors then found themselves in another river full of crocodiles and hippopotamuses. They had probably reached a fork in the Senegal River—the only river in this part of Africa where these animals are found.

The ships sailed back down the river and returned to Cerne. Then

they headed south again. Fourteen days later they reached the estuary of the Gambia River, where they stopped to take on supplies of water. After another five days' sailing, they landed on an island in a large bay. This was probably one of the Bissagos Islands off the coast of what is now Portuguese Guinea. There they found a salt lake that contained a smaller island. "We made our way there. In the daytime we could see nothing but forests, but at night we saw many fires. We heard the sound of pipes and cymbals, the rumble of drums and mighty cries. This instilled fear in us, and our soothsayers ordered us to leave the island." This account is the earliest description of the beating of African tom-toms. The arrival of the expedition probably coincided with a festival, for even today Hanno's description still fits such events.

Hanno continues: "We passed with great speed, and sailed along a burning yet sweet-smelling region where streams of fire ran out into the sea. We could not go ashore because of the heat. In the grip of fear, we made all haste from this place also. On the four nights following we saw land covered in flames. In the center of the land was a high pyre, larger than the others, which seemed to reach to the stars. In the daytime it proved to be a high mountain which is called the Chariot of the Gods."

The "land covered in flames" which apparently frightened Hanno and his sailors has a simple explanation. Along the Guinea coast it was an annual occurrence after the harvest for the farmers to burn loose straw and stubble to prepare the ground for the next year's planting of grain. But the "Chariot of the Gods" is not so easily explained.

Above: a beautiful necklace of glass beads and gold, of Carthaginian design. Hanno probably took various trading goods with him on his voyage, and used them to barter with friendly peoples he met. Glass beads were almost always included among such goods, but a finely-wrought necklace such as this would have been considered too precious for trade with primitive peoples.

Possibly Hanno was describing the volcanic Mount Cameroon in eruption, but it is difficult to understand how he could have got as far south as Cameroon in the sailing time he mentions. Another explanation is that Hanno and his crew saw Mount Kakulima, near the frontier between Guinea and Sierra Leone, with its slopes ablaze for some reason.

During the voyage Hanno probably tried to trade with friendly inhabitants along the coast. The Carthaginians developed a method of silent barter for which they became well known in Africa, and which later explorers have found extremely useful. The first move was made by the visitors. They landed on the coast, unloaded their cargo, and laid it along the water line. Then they lit a fire and returned to their ships. The Greek historian Herodotus describes the next stages: "The people of the country see the smoke, and, coming to the sea, they lay down gold to pay for the cargo and withdraw away from the wares. Then the Carthaginians disembark and examine their gold; if it seems to them a fair price for their cargo, they take it, and go on their way; but, if not, they go aboard again and wait, and then the people come back and add more gold till the ship's crew are satisfied."

But there was no chance of silent barter for Hanno at the most southerly point of his voyage. Three days after seeing the Chariot of the Gods, Hanno landed on an island. This may have been Sherbro Island, off the coast of Sierra Leone, although it was possibly as far south as Cameroon or even Gabon. The inhabitants of the island, like the people of Senegal, greeted Hanno and his men with stones. But these "forest dwellers" were very strange. Hanno says that they were mainly "women with long-haired bodies, and our interpreters called them 'gorillas.' We pursued them, but were unable to seize any because they fled and climbed steep cliffs and defended themselves with stones. We captured three women, but they bit and scratched their captors and would not go with them."

It has been suggested that Hanno may have been describing Pygmies, who have yellow skins, red-brown woolly hair, and hairy bodies. But were these "forest dwellers," in fact, human beings at all? The most likely explanation is that the unfriendly islanders were chimpanzees, smaller than gorillas and tailless. But Hanno obviously thought them human or he would hardly have used the word "women" in his report of their capture. And they must have been unusual trophies, for he adds, "We killed and skinned them, and took the hides to Carthage with us."

Hanno's account of this remarkable voyage ends abruptly. "We did not journey farther than this," he says, "since our provisions were beginning to run low." There is no record of the return journey, but Hanno and his crew would certainly have stopped to see how the settlers in each of the new colonies were faring. History tells little of the development of these colonies in the years and decades that followed. There are no accounts of subsequent visits by other navigators or of regular trade with Carthage. Of all the places

Below: during the last stop of his journey, on an island off the African coast, Hanno encountered some very strange people. He described them as "forest dwellers" and obviously thought they were human. The most likely explanation is, however, that these "forest dwellers" were chimpanzees. The Carthaginians would never have seen such animals before, and their similarity to human beings could well have led the sailors to believe that the apes were human.

mentioned by Hanno, only Cerne appears to have become important, probably because it was dealing in gold. Even this trade ended with the fall of Carthage in 146 B.C. Neither the Greeks nor the Romans seem to have profited from Hanno's great pioneering achievement.

For nearly 2,000 years, the stretch of West African coast explored by Hanno sank back into oblivion, from which it did not emerge again until the late Middle Ages. Then the Portuguese took half a century to rediscover the places that the Carthaginians had found and colonized in a few months.

# The Greek Adventurers
# 5

Even after he had landed the last of his settlers on the African coast, Hanno continued his journey southward. What made him go on? He had done what he set out to do. Now he was leading his men farther into unknown waters and possibly into danger. Yet he continued just the same. His reason can only have been a desire to know what lay beyond the horizon.

Hanno was experiencing the excitement of discovery—the lure of sailing unknown waters and seeing unknown places. Up to his time travelers nearly always had a good, practical reason for their journeys. They wanted to establish colonies or trade. Now there was another motive—the spirit of adventure. That spirit was given an added boost with the emergence of the Greeks as a great seafaring people.

A glance at a map showing their colonies in the 500's B.C. reveals that the Greeks were great sailors and persistent explorers. Already they were rivaling the Phoenicians. As well as establishing trading settlements, they, too, were starting colonies and building independent city-states where enterprising men emigrated with their families to start a new life.

A desire for freedom, a love of adventure, a curiosity about the

unknown—all these factors combined with economic necessity to make them migrate. It led them to rediscover areas which the Phoenicians, with their anxiety to safeguard their trade routes, had done so much to keep secret. By 500 B.C., the Greeks had established ports all over the Aegean and central Mediterranean. They had crossed to North Africa, and colonized Cyrene on the coast of present-day Libya. They had spread to the eastern extremities of the Black Sea, and as far west as Malaga in Spain. They had even ventured beyond the Strait of Gibraltar which was then called the Pillars of Hercules. They infiltrated Egypt, and established a Greek trading center in the Nile Delta. This caused a contemporary writer to complain that "the islands were restless." The Greeks, he went on to say, "were disturbed among themselves; they poured out their people all together. No land stood before them . . . they advanced upon Egypt. . . ."

Although it is known that more than a hundred Greek colonies existed, no descriptions have survived of the voyages that led to their foundation, and historians have been unable to discover exactly when these voyages took place. The sagas of the great Greek poet Homer—the *Iliad* and the *Odyssey*—probably provide indirect

Above: Odysseus and his men embark on their voyage home from the Trojan War, shown here in a picture from an Italian manuscript of the 1300's. In Homer's poem, the *Odyssey,* Odysseus was the king of Ithaca and a Greek leader in the war. It took him 10 adventure-packed years to reach home. Below: head of a Libyan from Cyrene.

65

accounts of the early Greek journeys. The legendary travels of Homer's hero Odysseus, which are so minutely described that they may well have a basis of truth, seem to speak for the wanderings of all the sailors of ancient Greece.

The existence of Greek colonies is mentioned in passing by Herodotus in about 450 B.C. and by Strabo, a Greek historian and geographer who lived around the time of the birth of Christ. But, by the time these authors were writing, some of the settlements had been in existence for hundreds of years. The details of their establishment had been forgotten. The brief references to Greek colonization made by these historians are supplemented by buildings which have survived and by archaeological finds. The magnificent temples at Paestum in southern Italy and Agrigento in Sicily, which are believed to date from around 600 B.C., provide evidence of Greek expansion. So do the hoards of Greek coins found at Marseille—the

former Greek colony of Massalia—on the southern coast of France.

Some of the colonizing voyages must have been dramatic and daring, but the colonies really owed their existence to exploration spread over centuries. As the years passed, mariners learned about the Mediterranean and the sailing conditions there, and they passed their knowledge on to the would-be colonists. From the various accounts of early sailors, the settlers could build up for themselves a reasonably accurate picture of the lands they were aiming for, and the sea they would have to cross to reach them.

The first Greeks are thought to have come from the steppe lands of southern Russia soon after 2000 B.C. Displacing the Pelasgians and other native inhabitants, they settled in groups of villages on the Greek mainland and the islands of the Aegean Sea. During the centuries that followed, they were increasingly influenced by the civilizations of Crete and Phoenicia, whose traders were frequent

Above: Stonehenge in Great Britain, which resembles the buildings of the distant Mycenaeans in the way the stones were cut and erected. At the peak of their power, the Mycenaeans were a great seafaring nation.

Above left: a wall-painting of Greek soldiers from Paestum, Italy. Paestum was the most northerly settlement the Mycenaeans made in Italy, commanding a wide agricultural area. But it had no strategic advantage, and was soon taken over by the Italians.

visitors to the southern shores of Greece. Gradually the Greek villages grew into cities. The largest and most important of these was Mycenae in the Peloponnesus (the peninsula forming the southern part of mainland Greece). Mycenae became so rich and powerful that, by about 1500 B.C., it was challenging the might of Crete itself.

In the next 200 years, the Mycenaean Greeks developed into a great seafaring nation. They traded throughout the Aegean and exported their wares to Egypt and Asia Minor (the peninsula of western Asia between the Black Sea and the Mediterranean, which is now occupied by Turkey). It is probably to this period of Mycenaean power that many of the Greek legends of seafaring heroes belong. But there followed a confused period of invasion and migration that gradually sapped the strength of the Mycenaean civilization. By the end of the 1200's B.C., Mycenae was in decline.

Left: after 2000 B.C., many peoples moved through Greece. This picture of warriors setting out comes from a vase dated around 1200 B.C., near the traditional date of the Trojan War.

Below: the Marble Street in Ephesus, one of the Ionian cities established in Asia Minor. Ephesus was a wealthy place—the fabulous Temple of Artemis (Diana) was one of the Seven Wonders of the Ancient World.

By the 1100's B.C., a number of migrating peoples had found their way into mainland Greece. Aeolians from the north moved into east central Greece and, in the Peloponnesus, other migrants settled and intermarried with the inhabitants to form a group known as the Ionians. In the late 1100's B.C., the Aeolians and Ionians were driven out in turn by a great wave of invading Indo-European tribes called the Dorians. These people, who were probably of much the same racial origin as the earliest Greeks, swept across the Greek mainland, conquering most of the Peloponnesus, and finally destroying the city of Mycenae.

It was with the invasion of the Dorians that the first great era of Greek colonization began. Fleeing before the invaders, Ionian and Aeolian refugees crossed the Aegean to the shores of Asia Minor, where they founded new settlements. Three hundred years later, there was another exodus when the population grew so large that Greece could no longer produce enough food for all its people. Economic shortages, together with a desire for freedom, drove the Greeks to emigrate throughout the Mediterranean and Black seas.

Sometime after 750 B.C., the Ionian Greeks established 12 cities in Asia Minor, which they organized into a confederacy. At Ephesus, they built the Temple of Artemis (Diana), one of the Seven Wonders of the Ancient World. Miletus, in Asia Minor, was the richest city in the Greek world until the 400's B.C., and the Greek city most concerned with exploration. It was at Miletus that the first maps and writing on navigation were produced. From its harbor sailed the ships that ventured into the Black Sea to trade with the nomadic Scythians of southern Russia.

So extensive was the colonization of Sicily and southern Italy, that this area was given the name of Magna Graecia. Places such as Naples, Messina, Syracuse, and Ischia owe their existence to the migrations of the Greeks after the middle of the 700's B.C. Present-day Antibes, Monaco, and Marseille were three among innumerable

Greek towns which dotted the Méditerranean coasts of what are now France and Spain as far west as Alicante.

Marseille (Massalia to the Greeks) was a colony of a colony. It was founded in about 600 B.C. by the inhabitants of Phocaea, yet another Greek settlement on the coast of Asia Minor. It is not surprising that the Egyptians, contemplating all this activity, described the Greeks rather sourly as "restless." They had firsthand evidence. There was a Greek colony, known as Naucratis, right in the Nile Delta.

The Greeks were lucky as well as restless. Prosperity grew out of a minor disaster that overtook one of their sea captains named Colaeus in 630 B.C. On a voyage from the Aegean island of Samos to Egypt he was swept off his course. An east wind drove his ship across the Mediterranean and past the Pillars of Hercules. Thus he became the first Greek to penetrate the narrow gateway into the "outer sea"—the Atlantic Ocean.

Above: a fragment of pottery with the autograph of Herodotus on it. It was found at Naucratis, where travelers used to write their names on vases, just as people today sign the visitors' book when stopping at a monument.

Colaeus brought his ship safely to shore at Tartessus, in southern Spain, where he sold his cargo. He carried back the news of what he had seen to Asia Minor, and for the next hundred years the Greeks benefited from his accidental discovery. The Phocaean Greeks opened up the silver trade from Spain to the Aegean with organized expeditions in 50-oared galleys. Marseille was obviously founded to serve as an intermediate port of call during these voyages.

Even more important than the penetration into the Atlantic was the gradual exploration of the Black Sea, the inland sea which,

Above: a gold buckle which belonged to Darius I of Persia. The Persian Empire retained its wealth and splendor until it was conquered by Alexander the Great in the late 300's B.C.

Right: the tomb of Darius I of Persia in the center of the cliff at Naqsh-i-Rustam, near Persepolis in what is now Iran. Darius' conquests greatly enlarged the Persian Empire.

because of its dense fogs and winter ice, the Greeks called the *inhospitable sea*. Even getting to it was difficult. Greek sailors had to learn to navigate the treacherous narrows of the Bosporus and the Dardanelles, which lie between the Aegean Sea and the Black Sea. For nine months of the year, strong currents run through these straits, backed by fierce northeast winds.

Exploration of the Black Sea probably began in the period between the 1100's and the 800's B.C. when the Carians, who occupied a region known as Caria in the southwest of Asia Minor, established colonies on its northern and western shores. But the Carians left no records of their voyages, and it was the people of Miletus who began the true opening up of the Black Sea in the 700's B.C. Tradition has it that the first settlements of people from Miletus were on the Dardanelles and the northern coast of what is now Turkey. From there, the colonists exported fish, metal, and wheat. They also possessed a far more exotic commodity—golden fleeces. These fleeces, which explorers brought back from the Caucasus, were produced by hanging sheepskins in gold-bearing streams, so that particles of gold clung to the wool. The sheepskins (fleeces) were later burned and the gold

was recovered. Here legend and fact may well go hand in hand. One of the most famous of the Greek myths tells the story of Jason, who sailed to the land of Colchis in search of the golden fleece. Colchis lay on the shores of the Black Sea, and it is possible that mariners' tales of the golden fleeces of the Caucasus could have given rise to the legend of Jason's golden fleece.

The first recorded exploration by a Greek mariner was made in about 510 B.C. By this time, the Greek colonies in Asia were under Persian domination, and it was on behalf of King Darius I of Persia

Below: a horseman in the costume of the Scythians, a group of nomads who lived in the region of the Black Sea. By 300 B.C., when this statue was made, the Greeks had known the area for nearly 400 years, and Greek influence is apparent in this work.

that the voyage was undertaken. Darius ruled an empire that stretched from Thrace in the Balkan Peninsula and Cyrene in northern Africa to northeast India. He was curious to learn the course of the Indus River, of which he knew only the upper reaches. To discover where the river entered the sea, Darius commissioned a Carian Greek named Scylax to sail down the Indus to its mouth. According to Darius' orders, Scylax was then to continue westward into the Arabian Sea, across the entrance to the Persian Gulf, and sail around Arabia and up the Red Sea to Egypt, which had been conquered by the Persians in about 525 B.C.

At the time when Scylax made his journey, the Greeks knew very little about the Red Sea or the Arabian Sea. Until about 600 B.C., the Egyptians had denied them a passage through the Red Sea and the Arabians blocked shipping farther eastward. Although sea routes from India to Arabia had probably been explored before, Scylax is the first Westerner who is known to have made the voyage.

Scylax came from the town of Caryanda, to the south of Miletus in Asia Minor, and was probably a commander in the Persian fleet. He probably traveled overland from Asia Minor to India, and built his ship at the point where the Indus becomes navigable. That is about 1,400 miles from the Indian Ocean.

Herodotus, the only recorder of the voyage, says that Scylax sailed down the river "toward the east and the sunrise." But this is inaccurate. The Indus makes its way south-southwest through what is now Pakistan. This might seem to throw doubt on the authenticity of the whole account, except for the fact that, when Herodotus was writing, the shape and size of Asia were unknown. He still thought of the world as a disk, and it was natural for him to visualize so distant a river as flowing east toward the outer edge of the disk.

Scylax left no account of his journey, but he is assumed to have been responsible for several strange tales about the peoples of India that were repeated by later writers. He came back with descriptions of the Shadowfeet People who used their feet to ward off the sun, of people who slept in the shelter of their own huge ears, and of men with only one eye. Of more scientific value was his success in completing his 2½-year voyage down the Indus, around southern Arabia, and up the Red Sea.

Once Darius knew that a sea route existed between his eastern domains and Egypt, he ordered the clearing of the old canal that linked the Red Sea with the Nile, and marked the event by raising a monument on its banks which proclaimed that ships "sailed through it from Egypt all the way to Persia as was my will."

More than a hundred years after the epic voyage of Scylax, another Greek, this time a soldier, led a land and sea expedition that ranks as one of the greatest feats in history. Xenophon brought 10,000 Greeks from the middle of the Persian Empire back to their native land.

Xenophon was an Athenian, a man of action, and a historian. By

Above: a seal showing Jason carrying the Golden Fleece. This famous legend may be based partly on fact—the Greek colonists in the Caucasus traditionally produced golden fleeces.

Above: a man with huge ears, one of the fabulous people apparently based on Scylax's tales. These stories had a powerful influence on the imagina- tion of western Europe. When the book containing this woodcut was published in 1544, the tales were still thought to be true.

the time he was 20, he had fought in battle and studied under the philosopher Socrates. Though skeptical about Athenian democracy, he was extremely patriotic and wanted to see Greece united against the Persian Empire. This aim, combined with the hope of possible honor and booty, led him to Asia Minor. There, he joined an army of Greek mercenaries being raised by Cyrus against Cyrus' brother, Artaxerxes II of Persia.

The army left Sardis (near present-day Izmir, in eastern Turkey) and marched southeastward through the mountains of Cilicia, past Aleppo in northwestern Syria, and down the Euphrates River into Babylonia. The Greeks covered a distance of about 1,700 miles in five months. At Cunaxa, on the Euphrates River north of Babylon, they routed the Persians, but Cyrus was killed, and the army, far from home and stranded deep in unknown country, elected Xeno- phon to lead them back to Greece.

To avoid returning by the same long overland route through Asia Minor, Xenophon decided to strike north and try to return to Greece by way of the Black Sea. Even today, with a knowledge of the country, and modern equipment such as maps, compasses, and mechanized transportation, such a journey would be formidable. In 400 B.C., to lead 10,000 battle-weary and dispirited soldiers and their camp followers on a 2,000-mile journey was a feat little short of superhuman.

Xenophon's route took the Greeks northward up the east bank of the Tigris River to Nineveh (about 230 miles north of present-day Baghdad, in Iraq), and then through the mountains of Armenia. To avoid attack from hostile inhabitants, they traveled over trackless hills. During the winter, they had to march through snowstorms, and at times wade waist-deep in rivers and mountain torrents. Exposed to bitter conditions and extreme hunger, many did not finish the journey. In his memoirs, Xenophon recounts that some lost toes through frostbite and others were blinded by the snow. He urged his men on, forbidding them to rest except at night. Before they slept, he ordered them to remove their footwear, so that their shoes would not freeze to their feet.

Once, the army made the mistake of taking a wrong route. For seven days they marched along the banks of a river, believing that it was carrying them toward the Black Sea. Then to his horror, Xenophon learned that he had been misled because two different

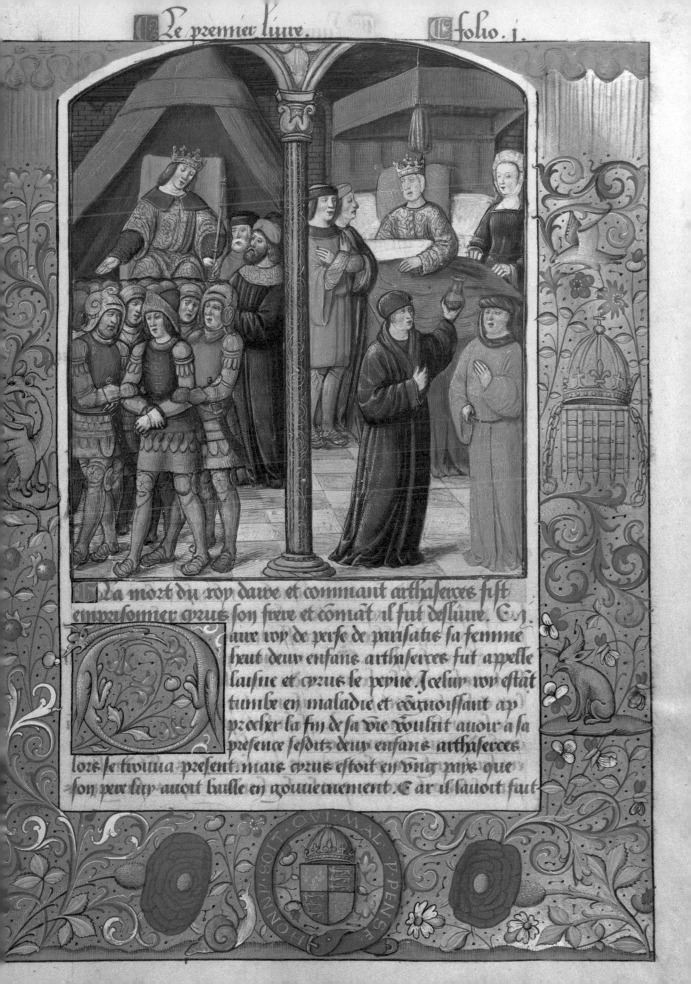

La mort du roy dauie et comment arthaſerces ſiſt
emprisonner cyrus son frere et comant il fut desliure. Ci
...aire roy de perse de pariſatis ſa femme
heut deux enfans arthaſerces fut apelle
laiſne et cyrus le puiſne. Icelui roy eſtāt
tumbe en maladie et conoiſſant ap
procher la fin de ſa vie voulut auoir a ſa
preſence ſesditz deux enfans arthaſerces
lors ſe trouua preſent. mais cyrus eſtoit en vng pais que
ſon pere luy auoit baille en gouuernement. Car il ſauoit fait

Left: Xenophon and his soldiers, an illustration from a French translation of his book made in the early 1500's. Xenophon is shown wearing a helmet, at the head of his men.

Right: Xenophon and his men on the shores of the Black Sea. The terrible 2,000-mile march had required every ounce of determination his weary men could muster. They had their reward when they saw the silvery gleam of the waters of the Black Sea in the distance. The Greeks believed that wherever there was salt water, the Greek language would be understood, and their way home certain.

rivers had the same name. The men were traveling in entirely the wrong direction. Weary and dispirited, they had to retrace their steps.

After a year of forced marches, local battles, and intense privation, the leading troops came to the head of a mountain pass. Xenophon, who was then with the rearguard, saw them waving their arms and heard excited shouts. Fearing that his men had been ambushed, Xenophon rode forward. Then he distinguished their cry: "The sea! The sea!" The army was at last within sight of its goal. Seven days later, Xenophon and his men reached the southeast coast of the Black Sea at Trapezus (Trabzon).

So Xenophon led his great army on the last stage of its journey. At Byzantium (Istanbul), on the Bosporus, he said good-by to his soldiers. He had brought them home through 2,000 miles of unknown and hostile territory. He had earned his future retirement with his wife and sons in Greece. There, on his country estate, he set a precedent for many future generals by writing his war memoirs. He gave them the modest, almost deprecating, title of *Up-Country March,* and possibly in terms of pure exploration the results were meager. But he had been where no Greek had traveled before and had taken notes of the country through which he had passed. His astonishing journey meant that more accurate maps could now be drawn. Xenophon had made a valuable contribution to the growing storehouse of geographical knowledge.

76

# Alexander the Great

# 6

In 356 B.C., about the time of Xenophon's death in Corinth, a boy destined to become one of the greatest generals history has known was born at Pella, in Macedonia. The boy was named Alexander. History calls him "the Great." He was the son of King Philip II of Macedonia, an outstanding military leader and administrator, and Queen Olympias, a brilliant and ambitious woman. While Alexander was growing up, Philip was fighting to extend Macedonian power down into Greece, and to bring the Greek city-states under Macedonian rule. He aimed to lead a united army from Macedonia and the Greek city-states against their common enemy, the Persians, who were in control of the Greek colonies in Asia Minor. Philip was murdered before this could be accomplished, but Alexander was ready for the task. He was determined to follow his father's plan and free the Greeks in Asia from their Persian masters. He set out to conquer the Eastern world, and he founded an empire of $1\frac{1}{2}$ million square miles which stretched from Greece to India and included Egypt, Asia Minor, and Persia.

Alexander's success as a military leader was extraordinary. But he was not content with conquest alone. During the 11 years in which he created a vast new empire, he combined the role of explorer with that of conqueror. He possessed the one quality essential to the explorer—an insatiable curiosity about the unknown world.

Left: the head of Alexander the Great. This head is known as the Azara Herm. It is a Roman copy, made in the late 300's B.C., of a portrait head by the Greek sculptor Lysippus.

Right: a pebble mosaic from Pella, the city where Alexander was born, showing the young Alexander hunting a lion.

79

Above: a page recounting a battle, from an illustrated edition of the *Iliad* dating from the A.D. 300's. The *Iliad*, like the *Odyssey*, is probably by the Greek poet Homer, and tells a story of the Trojan War. The work was obviously significant to Alexander, who carried a copy with him throughout his long travels.

As he penetrated deeper and deeper into the Orient, he sent back accounts of what he saw. Geographers, naturalists, and an official historian were important members of Alexander's staff. The writings of these scholars are now lost, but they were incorporated in the history of Alexander written by Arrian in the A.D. 100's. Some of their reports were also sent to the great Greek philosopher Aristotle.

Aristotle had been a leading influence in Alexander's education. King Philip had brought him from Athens to Pella when his son was 14. For three years, the philosopher had taught Alexander history, religion, science, and the theories of politics and monarchy. Together they read the Greek dramatists. Alexander was particularly influenced by the *Iliad*. He owned a copy of this work—marked with Aristotle's own notes—which had been given him by his teacher, and he carried this volume of Homer with him throughout his travels.

At the age of 20, Alexander succeeded his father as king of Macedonia. His father had died before the Greek states were completely subdued to Macedonian rule, and Alexander spent the first two years of his reign in making his authority felt in Greece. Then,

at last, he was able to turn his attention to the conquest of the Persian Empire. Early in the spring of 334 B.C., when he was 21 years old, Alexander set out on his great expedition. He was never to see his native country again.

Alexander's army consisted of 30,000 infantry and more than 5,000 cavalry. Along with his Macedonian troops were soldiers from Thrace and Thessaly, and men from many other Greek states. All the members of this force spoke some form of Greek. Alexander's troops made their first march at a speed which was to be characteristic of all their journeys. They covered the 300 miles to the Hellespont (Dardanelles) in only 20 days.

Once on the mainland of Asia Minor, Alexander visited the site of Troy, the ancient city made famous in Homer's *Iliad* and *Odyssey*. There, he made a sacrifice to the Greek goddess Athena and visited the supposed tomb of the legendary Greek warrior, Achilles, from whom he claimed to be descended. He exchanged some of his armor for a sacred shield said to have been used in the Trojan War. Thus, armed like one of the heroes of Greek legend, and believing himself

Above: Troy, which Alexander visited at the beginning of his campaign. The ruins of Homer's Troy were no longer visible by this time, and all Alexander would have seen was a small town. The archaeologists who have excavated the site of Troy have named the city of Homer's story Troy VIIa. Alexander's Troy is called Troy VIII.

to be more a god than a man, Alexander was ready to face the Persians.

During the first year of his campaign, he overcame the enemy in many battles, and won back for the Greeks the Persian-occupied cities of Ephesus, Miletus, and Halicarnassus. Then he marched on to Syria. He defeated Darius III, the king of Persia, in a great battle at Issus, near the Turkish-Syrian frontier. But, although Persian losses at Issus were enormous, Darius himself escaped. Alexander then pushed on to occupy Phoenicia, and laid siege to the city of Tyre. As in the past, Tyre put up a strong and determined

Right: a head of Ptolemy I, founder of an Egyptian dynasty which lasted from 323 B.C., until the death of Cleopatra in 30 B.C. Under the Ptolemies—as the dynasty was called —Alexandria became the intellectual and religious center of the world.

Left: a detail showing Alexander at the Battle of Issus, at the moment when Darius III decided to retreat. The mosaic was found in the House of the Faun at Pompeii, and is a copy of a painting of about 330 B.C.

resistance. While Alexander's troops were constructing a causeway across the half-mile of sea between the shore and the besieged island city, the Tyrians, perched high on their city walls, hurled missiles and red-hot sand down on the soldiers. On one occasion, a Tyrian ship ventured forth under the shelter of darkness and destroyed the part of the causeway that had already been built. It was only after seven months of laborious work and bitter fighting that the city finally fell to Alexander. With the capture of Tyre, which was the principal Persian port, Alexander became master of the Mediterranean.

Alexander was now free to travel south to Egypt, where he was crowned as pharaoh by a people grateful to be delivered from Persian rule. He visited the shrine of Zeus-Ammon, Egypt's chief god, at Siwah in the Libyan Desert, about 160 miles southwest of present-day El Alamein. There, the priests received him as the son of a god. On the edge of the desert, just west of the Nile Delta, Alexander founded the city that bears his name —Alexandria. Under Alexander's successors—the Greek Ptolemies—Alexandria was to become the chief city of the Mediterranean. With its renowned library containing 700,000 scrolls of parchment—the equivalent of 100,000 books—it grew into one of the most important cultural, as well as commercial, cities in the world. It was one of more than a hundred new cities, including 30 Alexandrias, that the young conqueror was to leave in his wake.

The next year was spent in pursuit of Darius. From Egypt, Alexander's army marched north again to Tyre, and then inland through Syria to the Euphrates and the Tigris rivers. At Gaugamela, near the ruins of the ancient Assyrian city of Nineveh, the Persians suffered their greatest defeat. But Darius constantly fell back across the desert plains and into the mountain regions of his immense empire. From Gaugamela, Alexander marched his army south through Babylon to the heart of the Persian Empire. There, he partially destroyed Persepolis, one of the great capitals of Darius.

Leaving Persepolis, Alexander followed Darius to Ecbatana (present-day Hamadan in Iran). The Greek Army covered an average of 36 miles a day, a punishing pace for the infantry. But Alexander never succeeded in catching the Persian king. In July, 330 B.C., somewhere near present-day Damghan (south of the Elburz Mountains), Darius was murdered by Bessus, a Persian general who

Right: Alexander, in Persian dress,
destroying idols, shown in a Persian
manuscript painting. Alexander's tact
in adopting Persian dress and many of
the Persian customs—although this
infuriated some of his men at the time
—helped establish him as a hero in
Persian legends long after his death.

Above: one of the surviving examples
of the elaborate stonework at Persepolis, the royal Persian city burned by
Alexander. This carving on a gateway
shows the Persian king fighting a lion.

ruled the province of Bactria in what is now northern Afghanistan.
Pausing only to take the title of king of Persia and assume Persian
dress (apparently to gain the good will of the local tribes), Alexander
went in search of the murderer who had also claimed the royal title.

This meant an autumn and winter march of 1,700 miles south into
Arachosia in Persia, and then northeast through the mountains to
Kabul in Afghanistan in the face of ice and bitter weather. Blocked
by snow, Alexander established a winter camp and waited until
spring before attempting to cross an 11,000-foot-high pass over the
formidable Hindu Kush mountain range. Once over the pass, the
army descended into the valley of the Oxus River (today called the
Amu-Darya). The river was swollen by melting snow, and the army
had no wood to build boats to cross it. Alexander ordered his men to
fill their leather tents with straw and use them as floats. By this means
the army crossed the Oxus into Sogdiana and caught up with Bessus,
whose supporters surrendered. Bessus himself was executed.

Now Alexander might well have called a halt to his expedition.
But he announced his intention of marching on to explore the northern borders of his new empire. The comparatively small army of
under 40,000 with which he had left Macedonia five years before was
now 200,000 strong. With seasoned troops and auxiliaries who had
either volunteered or been forced to join his army, Alexander
marched over 300 miles from the Oxus River to Maracanda (modern
Samarkand in the Soviet republic of Uzbek). Then, continuing
northeastward, he reached the great Jaxartes (Syr-Darya) River,
which had marked the northeastern boundary of the Persian Empire.

For two years, Alexander remained in central Asia, fighting and
exploring, marching and countermarching across the desolate plains
and uplands of present-day Afghanistan and the Uzbek and Turkmen regions of Russia. He toyed with the idea of exploring the
northern shores of the Caspian Sea to discover whether it was an
inland sea or the southern tip of a vast bay connected to the ocean
then believed to surround the world. But the unknown regions of
India attracted him more, and he turned his troops southward.

In the summer of 327 B.C., Alexander's men struck through the
Khyber Pass and reached the upper part of the Indus River. Some of
them plunged into the water for a refreshing swim. But, to their
horror, they found that the river was infested with crocodiles,
believed at that time to be found nowhere but in the Nile. Alexander

Below: the Indus River near Attock. It was near here that Alexander had a bridge built so that his army could cross the river. The Indus River was the first place at which his men found crocodiles, only previously known to live in the Nile, in Egypt.

began to wonder if this Indian river might somehow be joined to the Nile itself. After a few weeks' march over the plains of the Punjab in northwest India, the army arrived at another river, the Hydaspes (Jhelum), a tributary of the Indus. There, too, they found crocodiles. It therefore seemed to Alexander that both the Hydaspes and the Indus rivers must be the unknown sources of the Nile. He wrote a triumphant letter to his mother, announcing his great discovery. And he appointed a Cretan named Nearchus to build a fleet of ships, so that, whenever he chose, he could lead the army back to Egypt

and the Mediterranean by sailing down the Indus to the Nile.

It was not long, however, before Alexander realized his mistake. Local Indians told him that the Indus and Hydaspes flowed into the "great sea," a huge expanse of water that lay somewhere to the south. Greatly disappointed, Alexander destroyed the letter to his mother, although he did not call off the construction of the fleet. Still on the banks of the Hydaspes, Alexander then engaged in battle with Porus, the ruler of a land to the east of that river, and defeated Porus' huge army which included a contingent of 200 elephants.

As he pushed on into the Punjab, Alexander was at the extreme limit of the known world. Even the Persians had traveled no farther. But Alexander had heard reports of fertile lands and an immense river (the Ganges) to the east, and he could not resist the challenge of the unknown. His men were not similarly inspired. They had just marched through 70 days of incessant rain, and their morale was at a low ebb. They were weary of battles, and they felt that they had traveled far enough. After eight years away, they longed for home.

Alexander called his rebellious troops together and, in an eloquent speech, he urged them to go on. "I beseech you," he exclaimed, "not to desert your king just at the very moment he is approaching the limits of the inhabited world." Alexander had no idea of the vast plains of northern Asia stretching away to China. He believed, as Aristotle had taught him, that his army was almost at the boundary of the world, on the edge of the great outer ocean which he thought surrounded the entire earth. Soon, he told his men, they would reach the eastern sea which would be found to join up with the Caspian Sea, the Indian Ocean, and the Persian Gulf. He promised them that "from the Persian Gulf our fleet shall sail round to Libya, right up to the Pillars of Hercules."

But the soldiers stood in defiant silence. They would not go on. Reluctantly, Alexander gave the order for the expedition to turn around and march back across the Punjab. They returned to the Hydaspes, where Nearchus and a team of shipwrights (including Phoenicians, probably brought from Tyre) had almost finished constructing a large fleet of ships. For now Alexander had a new plan. He would explore the Hydaspes and the Indus to see if they issued into the great outer sea. Perhaps he might yet reach the boundaries of the world. Sending part of the army by land along the banks of the river to ward off hostile tribes, Alexander and the rest of his men embarked in a large number of 30-oared galleys and cargo ships. Without guides, and knowing nothing about the depth of the river or the conditions they might encounter, they made their way downstream. Ahead of them lay a voyage of about a thousand miles.

The fleet sailed down the Hydaspes and the Acesines (Chenāb) rivers and on to the Indus, fighting occasional battles along the way. Then, one day, they reached a point at which the river widened to about 20 miles, and they could smell sea air. Their joy at the thought that the ocean was not far off suddenly turned to anxiety

Below: a woodcarving made by the Kafiri, a red-haired, blue-eyed people from the mountains of what is now Afghanistan. The Kafiri claim to be descended from Alexander's Greeks. Marco Polo, who visited them in the A.D. 1200's, reported this as a certainty.

Above: Alexander the Great addressing his men in the hope of persuading them to continue farther into India with him. This painting, from a manuscript of the late 1400's, captures the sullen stubbornness of his men. By this time, the Greek soldiers were tired of travel, and only wanted to return to their homes in Greece.

as they found the current turning against them, and the fresh water of the river becoming salt. The salt water was being carried upstream by the rising tide. But the Greeks, used only to the almost tideless Mediterranean, knew nothing of the rise and fall of tides. They dropped anchor and waited for an improvement in the weather. While they were waiting, the tide ebbed and left their ships stranded. Alexander's men were terrified. They had never encountered such a phenomenon. And when the river rose again and set their ships afloat, they were even more amazed.

Shortly after this, Alexander sailed out into the open sea at the end of his nine-month voyage down the Indus. According to Arrian, he took a few ships down the western arm of the Indus Delta and sailed some way out into the Arabian Sea to discover whether any land was to be found in it. He then went back to Pattala at the head of the Indus Delta, where he had left the majority of his army. After a further expedition down the eastern arm of the delta, he returned to Pattala and divided his forces into three groups. The sick and the wounded were placed under the command of Craterus and ordered

to travel overland, with the baggage, to southern Persia. Alexander himself set out at the head of the main part of the army on a long march through hitherto unknown country along the shores of the Arabian Sea and the Persian Gulf. The rest of the troops, under the command of Nearchus, were sent by ship, with orders to explore the sea between the Indus Delta and the Persian Gulf. The plan was for Alexander to follow the coast and for Nearchus to touch land at various points so that Alexander's forces could supply the ships with food and water.

The plan failed. A range of hills forced Alexander's troops to make a detour away from the sea. This meant that Nearchus kept only one rendezvous with his commander during a voyage of 130 days from the Indus to the mouth of the Euphrates. The men at sea suffered from hunger and thirst as well as from exposure. From time to time, they landed but could find only the poorest of food.

One of Nearchus' most alarming experiences was an encounter with a school of whales. These creatures terrified the sailors, who had never seen a whale before. However, the monsters were successfully

Above: Alexander and his men caught in the tidal waters at the mouth of the Indus River. The Greeks, used to the almost tideless Mediterranean, could not understand why, near the mouth of the Indus, the current turned against them, and the water became salt. They were even more amazed when the tide went out, and left them stranded.

89

Right: the head of a man wearing a helmet of Grecian style, from a museum in Kabul, Afghanistan. Alexander's men took Greek art and culture with them to the lands they conquered, and the Greek influence persisted in Alexander's empire for many years.

Above: a vase decorated with Greek ships. These vessels are probably similar to those in which Nearchus and his men sailed from India to the Persian Gulf, while Alexander and his soldiers marched overland through the terrible Makrān Desert.

dispersed by a trumpet blast before they could damage the ships.

The problems facing Alexander on land were not so easily over come. The inland detour meant that, for two months, Alexander and his followers were marching through the arid wastes and shifting sand of the Makrān Desert (in present-day Pakistan). Water holes were scarce, and, faced with starvation, men began to kill pack mules for food. Three-quarters of Alexander's company died in the fearful journey before reaching Bandar-e Shāhpūr (in southeastern Iran). The survivors followed a caravan route that led inland from Bandar-e Shāhpūr towards Persepolis. On the way they were joined by Nearchus, whose joy at finding his commander again was dashed at the sight of Alexander's ragged and depleted forces.

It was a sad climax to the otherwise triumphant journey of exploration and conquest, a cruel ending to the march of 25,000 miles, which had been recorded with scientific precision by the *bematistae*—the *steppers*—as Alexander's road surveyors were called. Now only two years of life were left to the conqueror of the world. They were marked for Alexander by delusions of power and grandeur.

But, up to the time of his death at the age of 32, Alexander never lost his passion for exploration. He dispatched an expedition to explore the Caspian Sea. In the last few months of his life he made a personal voyage down the Euphrates River. He began assembling a great armada to sail to Arabia, which he intended to colonize. But

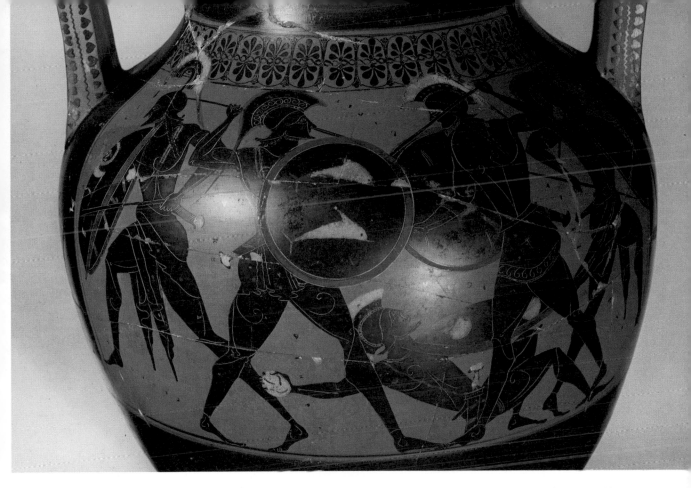

his plans were never to be realized. In the spring of 323 B.C., he fell ill with malaria. He died in the summer in the city of Babylon, which he had planned to make the capital of his great new empire.

Whatever his shortcomings in later life, Alexander's journeys confirmed him as one of the greatest explorers in history. Above all, he possessed a vision of what exploration could achieve in uniting a divided world. In 70 of the cities Alexander founded, Greek and Asian populations were deliberately mixed with the idea of uniting East and West into a single empire. At Susa (now in southwestern Iran), a year before he died, this internationalism took an even more personal form. This was a mass wedding in which 10,000 of his troops married Asian women, 80 of his Macedonian officers took Persian wives, and he himself took as his bride a daughter of Darius.

After Alexander's death, his empire was split up by his generals, and, before long, attacks from Gauls in the west and Parthians in the east divided it still farther. But Greek ideas and institutions continued to be a strong influence in the East. And the discoveries made by Alexander had vastly enlarged the known world of the Greeks. The lands that he had conquered or explored cover the modern countries of Greece, Bulgaria, Turkey, Iran, Afghanistan, West Pakistan, Iraq, Syria, Jordan, Israel, Egypt, and part of southern Russia. In the meantime, another Greek was pushing back the frontiers of the unknown in a different direction.

Above: a Greek vase, showing soldiers. The Greeks were used to difficult conditions, but even for them the march through the Makrān Desert was grueling. The heat and aridity of the region combined with hunger and thirst to cause many deaths among the men.

BLACK SEA

Thrace

3a from Pella

Byzantium
(Istanbul)

2A  2A

2

2A

2

2

Trapezus
(Trabzon)

CAUCASUS

CASPIAN SEA

HELLESPONT (DARDANELLES)

roy

ergamum

3a

2

Ancyra
(Ankara)

2

Sardis  3A

3a

3a

Euphrates

Gaugamela

Nineveh

2

Rhagae
(Teheran)

6

3A

3a

3A

GEAN

SEA

Ephesus

3A

3A

2

3a

2

2

Tigris

3a

Ecbatana

3d

3a

E L B U R Z

Miletus

3a

3a

alicarnassus

3a

2A

Issus

Aleppo

3a

3A

3d

3a

3d

3a

3a

3d

M E D I T E R R A N E A N

3a

3A

Damascus

Cunaxa

3d

3a

3d

Susa

Persepolis

3A

S E A

Tyre

Babylon

3d

Euphrates

5

3a

3d

probable former coastline

Alexandria

3a

3a

3a

3a

7a

P E R S I A N

3d

0

3a

siwah

1

Nile

L i b y a n

D e s e r t

5

G U L F

Hor

7c

7a

7b

7b

7c

7b

TROPIC OF CANCER

R E D

S E A

1

0°

1

30°

40°

50°

0     100     200     300     400     500
Miles

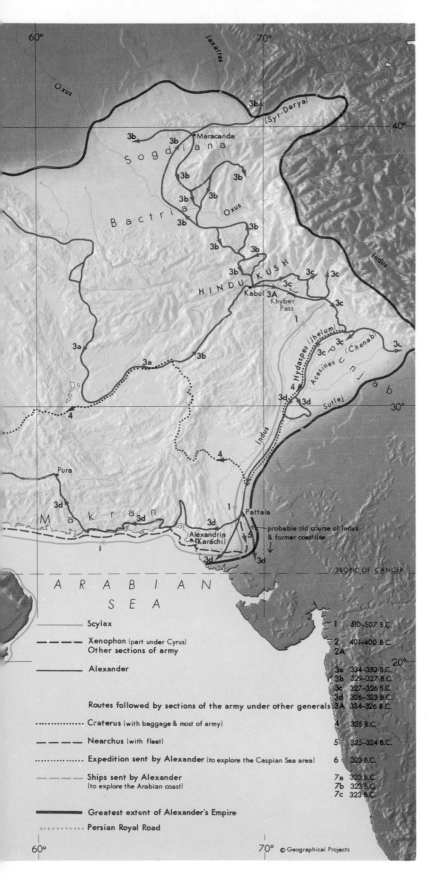

## Legend

| | | |
|---|---|---|
| Scylax | 1 | 510–507 B.C. |
| Xenophon (part under Cyrus) | 2 | 401–400 B.C. |
| Other sections of army | 2A | |
| Alexander | | |
| | 3a | 334–330 B.C. |
| | 3b | 329–327 B.C. |
| | 3c | 327–326 B.C. |
| | 3d | 326–323 B.C. |
| Routes followed by sections of the army under other generals | 3A | 334–326 B.C. |
| Craterus (with baggage & most of army) | 4 | 325 B.C. |
| Nearchus (with fleet) | 5 | 325–324 B.C. |
| Expedition sent by Alexander (to explore the Caspian Sea area) | 6 | 323 B.C. |
| Ships sent by Alexander (to explore the Arabian coast) | 7a | 323 B.C. |
| | 7b | 323 B.C. |
| | 7c | 323 B.C. |
| Greatest extent of Alexander's Empire | | |
| Persian Royal Road | | |

© Geographical Projects

Above: the death of Alexander, from a Persian manuscript entitled *Alexander's Celestial Journey*. With Oriental splendor, Alexander is shown being drawn to heaven by birds.

Left: the Middle East, showing the routes of the Greek explorers, from Scylax in 510 B.C. to Xenophon in 401 B.C., and Alexander the Great and his generals between 334 and 323 B.C. The frontiers of Alexander's empire at its greatest extent are also shown.

Left: a Greek statue of a man found at Massalia — present-day Marseille. Greek emigrants founded Marseille in about 600 B.C., and within 300 years the city had become an important cultural and commercial center. It was from Massalia that the great navigator Pytheas set out on his long voyage into the unknown northern waters.

Below: a coin from Marseille. On the reverse side is a lion and the word *Mazza*, a name sometimes given to the city of Marseille.

About the time that Alexander and Nearchus were setting out from the mouth of the Indus, a Greek explorer left Massalia (Marseille) in southern France. He sailed past the Pillars of Hercules, and headed for northern waters on a voyage that was to take him around the island of Britain. The explorer's name was Pytheas. His expedition, like that of Alexander in the eastern parts of the world, is a demonstration of the spirit of inquiry and adventure that prevailed throughout the Greek-speaking world.

Pytheas was a mathematician and astronomer as well as a great navigator. He was the first Greek to suggest that tides were dependent on the moon. He upset the prevailing belief that the Pole Star was the center of the heavens, and that all other stars revolved around it. Using a sundial, he calculated the latitude of his native Massalia with only a fractional error. Pytheas' scientific inquiries support the claim often made for him that he was the first scientific explorer in history. But it is unlikely that his travels were made solely in the interests of discovery. He visited the tin-mining areas of Cornwall, and challenged the Carthaginian monopoly of Atlantic sea routes—a matter of great concern to the Greek colonists of Massalia at this time. The Carthaginians had achieved supremacy in the Atlantic by blockading the Strait of Gibraltar. So successful had they been that Pytheas is the first Greek known to have reached the Atlantic since Colaeus was accidentally blown there 300 years earlier.

Pytheas' voyage was so exceptional that most early geographers and historians disbelieved and ridiculed his reports of it. He wrote a book with the modest title *About the Ocean,* and this seems to have been enough for him to be accused of telling travelers' tales. The book has been lost, but it is referred to by classical writers. The Greek historian Polybius, who saw the original, condemned the author as "an arch-falsifier." But this has been the reward of many explorers, and today Pytheas' account is largely accepted.

The date of Pytheas' voyage may reasonably be fixed at about 325 B.C. The kind of ship he sailed in is unknown. Unless the merchants of Massalia were backing him for commercial reasons, he is unlikely to have been able to afford a large one. But it must have been a vessel capable of standing up to a year's voyage of at least 7,000 miles (about the distance of Columbus' voyage to America and back) in far rougher waters than those of the Mediterranean.

From the fragmentary evidence available, it is impossible to tell

Below: cassiterite, crystals of tin ore. Cornwall was an important exporter of tin to the ancient world.

how Pytheas ran the Carthaginian blockade of the Strait of Gibraltar. He may even have avoided the strait altogether by traveling overland from Massalia on a trade route that ran north through France, and then sailing from Corbilo (St. Nazaire) at the mouth of the Loire River in northwest France. Alternatively, he may have slipped through the strait under cover of darkness and made his way around Cape St. Vincent, following much the same route as Himilco had done over 100 years before. His observations of latitude indicate that he passed what is now Oporto on the northwest coast of Portugal and continued northward through the Bay of Biscay to the island of Ushant off the tip of Brittany in northwest France. Leaving the French coast, he may then have struck across the English Channel directly to Land's End in Cornwall. Whatever his route, he passed beyond the northwestern limit of the world the Greeks knew as soon as he reached the waters north of Portugal. As he headed for the Cornish tin coast, he was making a daring trespass into the Carthaginian sphere of influence.

Once in Britain, Pytheas observed the way tin was extracted, smelted, refined, and cast into ingots for export. Then he probably rounded Land's End, and sailed up the west coast of Britain. There is no record that Pytheas landed in Ireland, but it is thought that he saw enough of the coastline to provide the Greek mathematician and astronomer Eratosthenes with the information he needed to locate it accurately on the map he drew a hundred years later.

Pytheas sailed all the way around Britain, which he judged to be triangular in shape. He placed Land's End (southwest England),

Right: ancient writers differ and modern historians disagree about the exact route followed by Pytheas, the Greek explorer, in about 325 B.C. This map of western Europe gives a number of possible routes and the places he may have visited on the way.

ARCTIC CIRCLE

THULE
(ICELAND)

ATLANTIC

OCEAN

FAEROE IS.

SHETLAND IS.

Duncansby Hd.

SCOTLAND

IRELAND

ENGLAND

Lands End

Cornwall

EN Foreland

ENGLISH CHANNEL

USHANT

Corbilo
(St. Nazaire) Loire

BAY OF

BISCAY

C. St. Vincent

S OF HERCULES
F GIBRALTAR)

NORTH

SEA

Helgoland

Rhine

Rhone

Massalia

Rhone

MEDITERRANEAN

SEA

BALTIC SEA

Scandinavia

ARCTIC CIRCLE

Miles

──────── 1  Pytheas' route according to Stefansson & Broche
─ ─ ─ ─   1a Areas where Broche differs from Stefansson

──────── 2  Pytheas' route according to Markham & Synge
─ ─ ─ ─   2a Return journey where Synge differs from Markham

──────── 3  Pytheas' route according to Russian authorities

· · · · · · 4  Pytheas' route according to Hermann

© Geographical Projects
24°

Above: an Anglo-Saxon map of the A.D. 900's, showing the ocean that was believed to surround the world. Although some Greek scholars had believed the earth to be round, the idea of a flat world surrounded by sea was again current by the A.D. 900's. It was to persist for centuries to come.

the North Foreland of Kent (southeast England), and Duncansby Head (northeast tip of the Scottish mainland) as the three extremities. He estimated the distance around Britain as 4,684 miles (double the real length of the coastline) and the distance across the English Channel from Dover in southeast England to Calais in northern France as 11 miles (instead of 21). These inaccuracies are part of the reason why Pytheas' account of his expedition is not always believed today. But the difficulties of measuring distances at sea in his time were considerable and many other sailors made similar mistakes.

Another misleading statement about Pytheas' voyage was made by Polybius, who says that the explorer "traveled all over Britain by foot." This probably means that Pytheas landed at various places where he was able to make important observations about the country and the people. He noted that the Britons stored grain in covered buildings because of the rain, and, for the same reason, threshed indoors. He found the country extremely cold and observed that the large population led a primitive existence, living in log and reed houses, eating simple foods, and drinking *curmi*, a type of beer.

To Pytheas' contemporaries, and to all geographers in the pre-Christian era, it was a matter of the greatest interest to learn how far north the world stretched. The notion that a sea—Oceanus—encircled the central land mass still persisted, and everyone was naturally curious to know where in the north sea and land would meet. Pytheas brought back an answer. He said that he had been told about an island called Thule. Six days' sailing from the north of Britain, this was the "outermost of all countries."

As an astronomer, Pytheas was fascinated by the information that

Above: ocean ice, now called pancake ice. Pytheas wrote that the sea beyond Thule (probably Norway or Iceland) was sluggish and congealed and that ships could not sail through it. This has been taken to mean that he encountered ocean ice. Pytheas described the ice as looking like a jellyfish.

Above: a coin of Euergetes II, who sponsored Eudoxus' voyage to India.

Right: a map showing Thule, which was first described by Pytheas. Whether Thule was what is now Iceland or part of Norway has never been determined.

in Thule the day was 24 hours long at midsummer. This indicates that Thule must have been either Norway or Iceland. But from the scanty information about Thule given by the writers who quote Pytheas, it is impossible to know for certain which of these two countries is meant. Pytheas is reported to have said that beyond Thule the sea became sluggish and congealed, and that men could neither sail through it nor walk over it. He also said that the inhabitants of Thule lived on wild berries and grain and made a mead-like drink from the honey of their bees. The congealed sea has been taken to refer to the sludge at the edge of the Arctic ice, which is more likely to be encountered off Iceland than Norway. Bees, however, are not found as far north as Iceland, and this has strengthened the belief that Thule was a part of Norway, even though Norway is not an island.

It is not certain whether Pytheas visited Thule, and little is known about the remainder of his travels. He may have followed the coast of Europe northeastward to explore beyond the Rhine. He is known to have landed on an island in northeast Europe where "in the Spring the waves wash up amber upon the shores." Perhaps this was Bornholm, 25 miles off the southern coast of Sweden. If so, Pytheas was the first man from the ancient world to enter the Baltic Sea. But the description could apply equally to the amber island of Helgoland off northwest Germany in the North Sea.

After Pytheas' return to Massalia, there were apparently no further Greek voyages to the north. The Carthaginians maintained their blockade on the Atlantic until Carthage fell to the Romans in 146 B.C. No one could verify Pytheas' discoveries, and this was certainly one of the reasons why his reports were open to the scorn of later historians.

Explorers' reports are a natural target for skeptics, and the story of Eudoxus, the first Greek to reach India by sea, was no exception. Eudoxus was a rich merchant from Cyzicus, a port in Asia Minor on the Sea of Marmara, which separates the Bosporus and the Dardanelles. His voyage was made in about 120 B.C. and started from Egypt. He was staying in Alexandria at the court of the Greek king of Egypt, Euergetes II, when some strange news was received. A shipwrecked Indian had been brought in from the Red Sea. He was nearly dead from drowning, but when he had been nursed back to health, Euergetes ordered that he was to be taught enough Greek to give an account of his voyage from his native country.

The rescued man's story was that he had been blown hundreds of miles from India across the Arabian Sea. This could not be corroborated as all his companions had been drowned. He insisted that they had been the victims of mischance, and if the king doubted the possibility of making such a voyage, he would readily act as a guide to take a ship back the way he had come.

Euergetes accepted the offer, and Eudoxus agreed to lead the expedition. With the Indian as his pilot, he set off down the Red Sea. All details of his voyage are lost, however. The story is wound up all

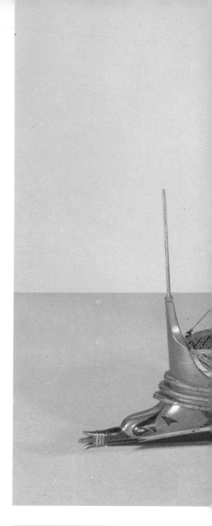

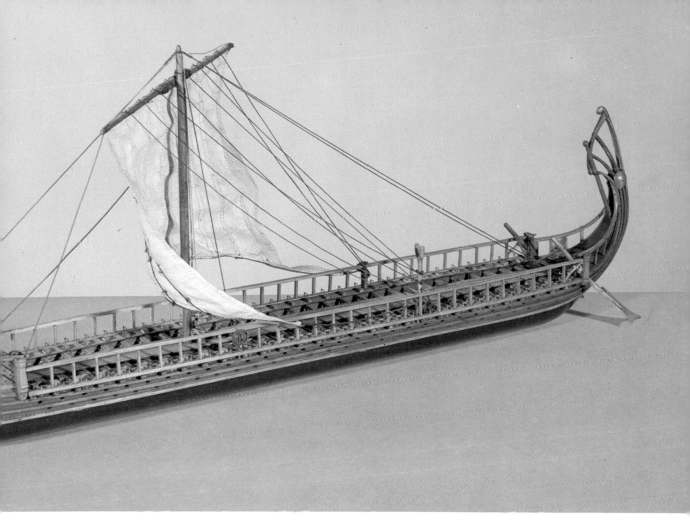

Above: a modern reconstruction of a Greek trireme—a ship like those probably used for the most ambitious Greek voyages. As no complete contemporary sculpture or painting of a trireme has been discovered, no one knows exactly what these ships looked like. It is known, however, that they were propelled by 170 oars in 3 banks, and were some 150 feet long

Left: rough and cut gemstones from India and Ceylon—sapphires, rubies, and garnets. These treasures of the mysterious East were a much-desired luxury for the Mediterranean peoples.

too briefly by the historian Strabo. He merely recounts that, after reaching India, Eudoxus "sailed away with presents, and he returned with a cargo of perfumes and precious stones. . . ." The pioneer explorer of one of the world's most important sea routes received no honors or rewards. According to Strabo, "Eudoxus was badly disappointed for Euergetes took from him his entire cargo." Possibly the historian was exaggerating Eudoxus' reaction, for in all such Egyptian state enterprises the king had a right to the cargo.

After the death of Euergetes, his wife Cleopatra, who had succeeded him as regent for their son Soter II, sent Eudoxus out again to India with several ships. On the homeward journey, Eudoxus was blown off his course and forced to land on the African coast below Cape Guardafui, in Somaliland. When he finally made his way back to Alexandria, all his cargo was once again taken from him.

Finding state voyages of such little profit, Eudoxus then embarked on a career of private exploration. While he had been on the African coast, he had found a wooden prow in the shape of a horse that had been washed ashore from a wrecked ship. The shipwrights of Alexandria told him that this was a figurehead from one of the small vessels of Gades that plied the West African shores as far as northwest Morocco. Since Eudoxus had found the prow on the East

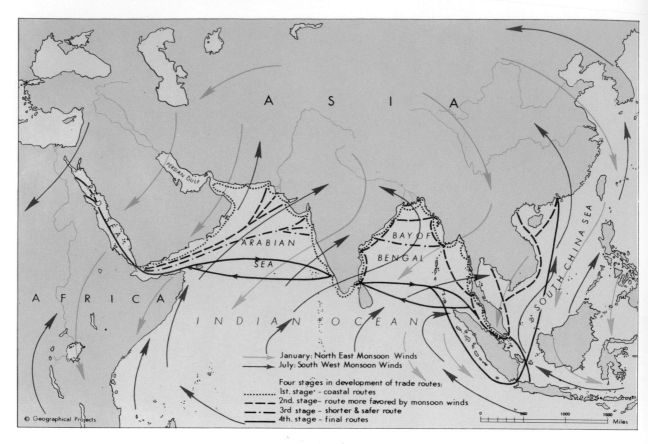

Above: this map of the Indian Ocean
shows the main direction of the
monsoon winds—northeast in January
and southwest in July. It also shows
how the sailors of the ancient world
used these seasonal winds to extend
their trade routes as far east as China.

African coast, he concluded that it was possible to sail around
Africa. He set out to try to reach India by rounding Africa from west
to east, but abandoned the voyage when his ships ran aground on
the Moroccan coast. Of his second attempt to circumnavigate
Africa, nothing is known. He left Gades in about 105 B.C. and was
never seen nor heard of again.

But Eudoxus' earlier voyages to India were not forgotten. For it
seems probable that he brought back information that made long
voyages across the open sea possible. The mysterious Indian guide
may well have shown Eudoxus how to make use of the southwest
summer monsoons. These winds would have blown the Greek
captain's ship straight across the Arabian Sea to his destination.
Eudoxus could then have used the northeast winter monsoon to
make the return journey. For centuries, Arabian and Indian sailors
had traveled between the Indian ports and the Red Sea with the aid
of the regular seasonal winds of the monsoon. Nearchus, Alexander's
lieutenant, had probably been the first Westerner to see the importance of these seasonal winds, which blow for six months from the
southwest and for six months from the northeast. But, as far as is
known, the Greeks of Nearchus' time ignored his discovery, and
continued to make their voyages hugging the coast. The importance
of the monsoons came as an immense revelation to Eudoxus.

Even after Eudoxus' discovery, the monsoon route to India was
at first little used. In fact, its discovery has also been attributed to a

Greek merchant called Hippalus who sailed from a port on the Red Sea to the Malabar Coast of western India in about 45 B.C., nearly 80 years after Eudoxus' voyage. The southwesterly monsoon even came to be called *hippalus* in his honor. But although Hippalus was not the first to use the monsoons to make his voyage, his journey played a vital part in establishing a trade route to India. Around the time of the birth of Christ, as many as 120 ships a year were using the monsoons to sail from Egypt to India across the open sea.

Before long, Greek sailors also found a more southerly route across the Arabian Sea to the southern tip of India and Ceylon. Venturing farther still, these unknown mariners made their way around India into the Bay of Bengal, and explored the east coast of India as far north as the mouth of the Ganges. In about A.D. 120, a merchant named Alexander is reported to have used the monsoon to sail across the Bay of Bengal from India to Malacca, on the Malay Peninsula. He then continued his voyage around the southern tip of the peninsula, across the Gulf of Siam and northward as far as the present-day frontier between North Vietnam and China.

If this is true, Alexander was the first man of the western world to open up a sea route to China. As with so many of the early discoverers, little is known about this daring sailor. But his remarkable achievement, and the pioneering voyages of those who first sailed the seas between Africa and India, have a place of honor among the world's great voyages of exploration.

Right: the head of the stone dragon Makara from the area that is now Vietnam. In about A.D. 120, a Greek merchant called Alexander opened up a sea route to China. This was the first recorded voyage to the Far East.

# Hannibal Crosses the Alps

# 8

Above: Hannibal, on a silver shekel struck at Cartagena around 220 B.C.

Left: Hannibal crossing the Alps. This illustration is taken from a manuscript made centuries after Hannibal's journey. The artist clearly knew little more about elephants than the Roman soldiers of Hannibal's own time, who had been terrified by the sight of these huge beasts.

In the temple of Baal Shamin at Carthage, a nine-year-old boy stood beside his father, the great general Hamilcar Barca. He placed his hand on a sacrificed animal and swore to take vengeance on Rome, the enemy of his country. The boy's name was Hannibal. And his oath was the prelude to the most daring and unorthodox expedition of early times—a 940-mile march that took an army of men and elephants across the Alps. This was a journey of such difficulty and appalling hardship that it could never have succeeded without the outstanding abilities and iron will of a man like Hannibal. He was a brilliant strategist, a great leader, and single-minded in the pursuit of his aims.

Hannibal was born in 247 B.C. and grew up when Carthage was engaged in a death struggle with Rome. For 250 years, the Carthaginians had been masters of the western Mediterranean. Now the supremacy of Carthage, the largest and richest city in the world, was challenged by the new military power that had grown out of a confederacy of Italian tribes. During Hannibal's boyhood and early manhood, there was a complete change in the old Mediterranean spheres of influence. When Hannibal was six, the island of Sicily was wrested from Carthaginian control by the legions of Rome. The fall of Sicily in 241 B.C. ended the 23-year struggle between Carthage and Rome known as the First Punic War. The Carthaginian Navy was wiped out. Carthage was forced to accept humiliating terms for peace and to pay huge fines to the Roman victors. In 239 B.C., threatened by a fresh outbreak of war, the Carthaginians ceded Sardinia and Corsica to Rome.

Carthage itself stood in danger, but the Carthaginians' determination to resist Roman domination did not weaken. Soon after Hannibal had made his sacred vow in the temple, he set out with his father for Spain, where Carthage was to found an extension of its empire. For Hamilcar had already conceived the daring plan of marching overland from Spain and striking at the Romans from the north. Rome could mobilize a large army at short notice. Surprise was therefore essential. But Carthage had no navy with which to launch a seaborne invasion of Italy. Nothing could, however, be more unexpected than the arrival of an army across the Alps. Before he could undertake such an expedition, Hamilcar had to build up a strong base in Spain, recruit men for his army, and obtain enough money to finance his campaign.

At first, Hamilcar made the old Carthaginian town of Gades (Cádiz) his base. But soon he began the systematic occupation of southern and southeastern Spain. Copper mines were opened and agriculture flourished. An advance base was established near Alicante on the east coast. Spanish tribes were incorporated into a growing colonial army. When an alarmed mission from Rome arrived to discover what was happening, they were told that all this was in Rome's best interest. Why, it would ensure Carthage's steady payment of war debts!

When Hannibal was 18, his father was drowned in the course of one of his expeditions. Hannibal, who had already proved himself an outstanding soldier, continued to serve under Hamilcar's son-in-law Hasdrubal, who founded the city of New Carthage (Cartagena) on the southeastern coast of Spain. When Hasdrubal was murdered in 221 B.C., the 26-year-old Hannibal was unanimously elected commander in chief of the army. For three years, Hannibal worked to build up his forces, and continued to increase Carthaginian power in Spain. In 219 B.C., he attacked the city of Saguntum, in eastern Spain, which was allied to Rome. After a bitter seven-month siege, Saguntum fell to Hannibal. Rome at once declared war on Carthage, and the Second Punic War began. The time had come for Hannibal's long-pledged expedition of revenge.

In the spring of 218 B.C., Hannibal marched out of Cartagena with an army of 60,000 infantrymen, 12,000 horsemen, and a troop of

Below: Hannibal as a young boy making his solemn oath to take vengeance on Carthage's enemy, Rome. Watched by his father, Hamilcar Barca, Hannibal swore on the body of an animal that had been sacrificed to the gods.

37 elephants. His departure bore a distinct resemblance to that of Alexander, 116 years earlier. Here was another son fulfilling the plans of his father, a young general intent on the conquest of his enemies. Ahead of him lay a five-month march from Spain to Italy across the Pyrenees, the Rhône River, and one of the highest passes in the Alps.

The elephants added to the difficulty of the march. But they had an important role to play in Hannibal's campaign. Elephants were the tanks of ancient warfare. Ever since they had first been encountered in battle by Alexander's troops on the banks of the Hydaspes, their value as a substitute for war chariots had been recognized. They were extremely valuable pack animals and, although their behavior in battle was unpredictable, they could be useful against enemy cavalry that had not been trained to meet them. But, above all, they were a powerful psychological weapon. Hannibal knew that his elephants would create panic among the Roman soldiers, who would never have seen such creatures before.

At the start of the expedition, Hannibal did not reveal to his troops that their destination was Italy. But when the army was preparing to cross the Pyrenees, a number of the men must have guessed the daunting prospect ahead, for they mutinied. Hannibal decided to leave behind 7,000 of the more unreliable men. With the remainder of his army, he pressed on over the Pyrenees and marched into southern Gaul (France).

Above: a Punic coin with the head of Hamilcar Barca, minted at Cartagena late in the 200's B.C. *Punic* was the Roman name for the people of Carthage – in Latin it means *Phoenician*.

Below: the Pyrenees, which divide France from Spain, and which Hannibal's men had to cross at the start of their long march. The exact route they took cannot be determined from the accounts of the expedition.

Hannibal could then have followed the coast all the way through Gaul along the present-day French Riviera to Italy, thus avoiding the hazards of the Alpine passes and shortening his journey considerably. But the Greek colony of Massalia (Marseille), which lay on this route, was allied to Rome, and might have called for help. A head-on collision with a Roman army between the Basses Alpes and the Mediterranean Sea was too great a risk for Hannibal to take. So the Carthaginian general struck north up the Rhône Valley well west of Marseille.

The crossing of the Rhône was the first serious natural hazard. It was probably made at Fourques just above Arles. At this point, the river was shallow and the current not too swift. But the river was three-quarters of a mile wide. Hannibal took five days to obtain boats from the local inhabitants and assemble a fleet of rafts for the infantry. Some of the horses were embarked on boats. Others were pulled through the water by the men in the boats. The remainder swam across with their riders.

Getting the elephants to the far side was not so easy. Two 100-foot-long piers were built out into the river and attached to large rafts. Piers and rafts were covered with earth so that the elephants believed they were still on land when they were led onto them. As the rafts were towed away, some of the elephants took fright and a number of rafts capsized. But the river was shallow enough for the

Above: Hannibal and his men crossing the Rhône River. Although the river was shallow and the current did not flow too swiftly, the crossing presented considerable difficulties.

Left: the reverse side of two Carthaginian silver coins, showing elephants. The elephants that accompanied Hannibal's army had been captured in the foothills of the Grand Atlas, Morocco.

elephants to wade across, keeping their trunks above the surface. All the elephants reached the far bank safely.

Historians who wrote of Hannibal's journey recorded no place names, and, as a result, his route over the Alps is subject to much speculation. Scholars have had to work mainly on the general descriptions provided by the Greek historian Polybius. He states that the actual crossing of the Alps took 15 days, and gives an account of each day's march. From the evidence provided by Polybius and other classical writers, the British historian Sir Gavin De Beer, whose book on Hannibal is the result of 40 years' research, concludes that Hannibal took the southern pass over the Col de la Traversette, east of the town of Gap.

According to Sir Gavin, after the crossing at Fourques, Hannibal followed the Rhône to a point north of Montélimar, where it is joined by the Drôme River. There, he turned his army east along the

Above: a detail taken from the above engraving, showing one of the rafts used to get the elephants across. The rafts were covered with earth so that the elephants would not be frightened.

valley of the Drôme, which winds its way to Die. Ahead lay the jagged peaks of the Alps, but Hannibal's troops were still traveling through valleys of trees and grassy slopes until they reached the Col de Grimone. In one of the low passes the convoy was attacked from above by a hostile local tribe. During the skirmish, Hannibal lost many animals which fell over the steep drop on one side of the narrow, uneven path.

After this encounter, which took place on the second day in the mountains, Hannibal's troops captured a town that was large enough to supply food for the men and forage for the animals. There Hannibal ordered a day's rest. But there was no time to waste. It was already October. The weather was getting colder and the ascent had still to be made into even more bitter altitudes. For two days after leaving the town all went well. But on the army's seventh day in the mountains, Hannibal was approached by more tribesmen.

These men came carrying olive branches to indicate peace, and offered guides. But Hannibal, suspicious of their intentions, put his elephants, cavalry, and pack animals at the front of the column, and his heavy infantry behind. This enabled him to fight a rearguard action when, just as he had anticipated, there was an attack. The enemy chose a narrow gorge with a wall of cliffs on one side and

a ravine on the other. They rolled down rocks on the Carthaginians, and for a while succeeded in splitting the column in two. But it joined up again, and, though he had suffered some losses, Hannibal pressed on.

The eighth and ninth days took him over the highest pass, 9,000 feet up and covered with snow. The going was hard and the troops were very near the end of their resources. Hannibal ordered a two-day halt to reassemble the convoy disorganized by the attack and to allow stragglers to catch up. Through gaps in the mountains it was possible to see the plain below, and Hannibal indicated to his men the direction of Rome. From now on, he promised them, the march was downhill and victory certain.

Above: "Snowstorm: Hannibal and his Army Crossing the Alps" by J. M. W. Turner (1775–1851). Turner was an English Romantic landscape painter, whose greatest works are studies of light, color, and atmosphere. As the title of this picture suggests, Turner was more interested in the snowstorm than in Hannibal. The figures of the Carthaginian conqueror and his men can barely be made out amid the swirling splendor of this fierce blizzard.

Above left: Punic armor of the type worn by Hannibal's soldiers. The pieces are decorated breast and back plates, with shoulder braces and belt.

But the descent did not prove as easy as he hoped. The track down which the column began to wind its way was narrow and covered by a deceptive layer of snow. A false step to one side by soldiers or pack horses, and they slithered to their death down a precipice. This was a constant danger. But worse was to follow. The front of the column suddenly came to a halt. The track had disappeared. A landslide had obliterated it over a distance of more than 200 yards. With great difficulty, Hannibal's men were just able to scramble across the gap. But, for the horses and elephants, progress was impossible.

There was no alternative but to clear the snow and repair the track. A particularly large rock that was lodged directly in their path

had to be removed. To do this, the men felled trees, cut them up, and lit a fire on top of the rock. Then they drenched the rock in vinegar or sour wine, until it split as a result of the heat and the chemical action of the acetic acid. Pickaxes did the rest. The way was cleared and sufficiently repaired for the army to make the final part of their descent onto the Italian plain.

The figures for Hannibal's losses from the time he crossed the Rhône until he reached Italy are conflicting. They have been placed as high as 36,000 men. This is an enormous number in proportion to the total strength of his army, which had already been considerably

Left: the struggle to remove rocks from the path on Hannibal's descent, shown in a drawing of the 1600's by Pietro da Cortona. In the background, the army clambers through a gorge.

Right: a bronze bust of the Roman general Scipio Africanus, who finally defeated Hannibal's army at Zama.

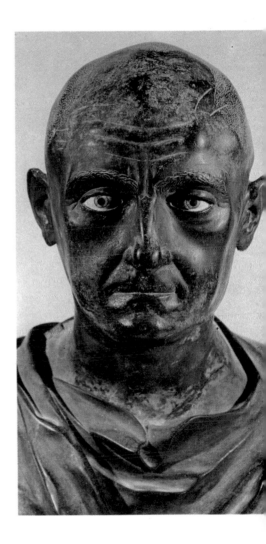

weakened by the time it reached the Rhône. The march was a triumph of endurance, and not least for the elephants. All of them are said to have survived the mountain journey, but, with no chance of getting natural foodstuffs at high altitudes, they suffered seriously. Considering the difficulties, it was also a triumph of speed. The 15-day journey through the mountains was achieved at an average speed of 9 miles a day, or, if the rest-days are deducted, 12 miles a day.

The rest of Hannibal's story belongs more to the history of war than to an account of exploration. The strategy of surprise suc-

ceeded. He won a series of great victories: first at the Trebia River in northwestern Italy; then, after crossing the Apennines, at Lake Trasimeno in central Italy; and then, in 216 B.C., at Cannae in the southeast, where the Romans suffered the worst defeat they had ever known. But although Hannibal remained in Italy for 15 years, he was never able to defeat the Romans decisively. After the Battle of Cannae, the armies met·in numerous skirmishes, but they never again joined in open battle. In the autumn of 203 B.C., Hannibal left

Italy on receiving urgent orders to return home. Carthage was under
siege by the Romans, and he was recalled to oppose the advance of
the Roman general Publius Cornelius Scipio (later known as Scipio
Africanus). Hannibal's army, so long undefeated on the Italian
mainland, at last met its match. It was crushed by Scipio at Zama
(Jama, 74 miles southwest of Tunis), and this defeat signaled the
beginning of the twilight of Carthage. Just over 50 years later, the
city was completely destroyed.

Hannibal did not live to see the end of the city to which he had
dedicated his life. In 183 B.C., he died by his own hand rather than
surrender to the Romans. Sometime before his death, he met the
man who had defeated him at Zama. Scipio asked him whom he
considered the greatest general in history. Without perhaps realizing
it, Hannibal named the one leader comparable with himself as a
military explorer. His reply was "Alexander the Great."

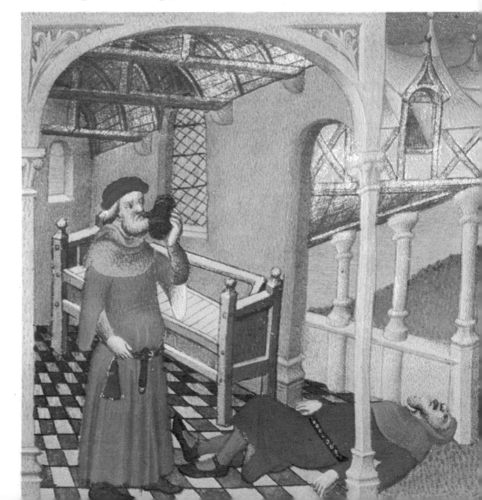

Right: Hannibal died by drinking
poison. This manuscript illustration
of about 1410 shows the famous general drinking the draught and, on the
right, his dead body. Hannibal
killed himself rather than face capture, saying, "Let us now put an end
to the great anxiety of the Romans,
who have thought it too lengthy
and too heavy a task to wait for the
death of a hated old man." Hannibal
was then 64 years old.

# Rome's Exploring Legions

# 9

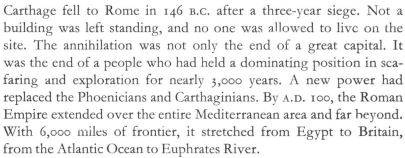

Carthage fell to Rome in 146 B.C. after a three-year siege. Not a building was left standing, and no one was allowed to live on the site. The annihilation was not only the end of a great capital. It was the end of a people who had held a dominating position in seafaring and exploration for nearly 3,000 years. A new power had replaced the Phoenicians and Carthaginians. By A.D. 100, the Roman Empire extended over the entire Mediterranean area and far beyond. With 6,000 miles of frontier, it stretched from Egypt to Britain, from the Atlantic Ocean to Euphrates River.

The first Roman emperor, Augustus, who ruled from 27 B.C. to A.D. 14, wrote: "My fleet sailed along the ocean from the mouth of the Rhine to the country of the Cimbri [a Germanic people] which no Roman before that time had penetrated by land or sea. . . . I advanced the boundaries of Illyria [in present-day Albania] to the banks of the Danube. . . . Many embassies were sent to the Indian kings . . . I added Egypt to my Empire. . . ." These were the achievements of a single reign. During the 200 years from 100 B.C. to A.D. 100, the Romans also explored Britain; they went in search of the source of the Nile; they crossed the Grand Atlas mountains in Morocco and marched to the Persian Gulf; and they journeyed to Yemen and into present-day Crimea.

This might suggest that the Romans were the greatest of all the early explorers. Certainly they brought law and order, government, and civilization to far countries. But not all their campaigns can be regarded as true exploration. Some were purely military expeditions, made with the sole purpose of conquest. In others, however, the Romans did push back the frontiers of the known world. Julius Caesar's famous words from Zela (Zile) near the Black Sea—"I came, I saw, I conquered"—sum up the dual role of the explorer-general.

The Romans went into Asia in 192 B.C., and extended their influence as far as the Taurus Mountains in the south of modern

Left: a cameo of Augustus, the first of the Roman emperors. Augustus came to power after the death of Julius Caesar, and ruled as emperor after 27 B.C. Under Augustus, the boundaries of the Roman Empire were expanded far beyond their previous limits. Here, Augustus is shown in godlike splendor as slaves are brought before him.

Overleaf: the Mediterranean Sea showing the frontiers of the two rival powers, Rome and Carthage, in 218 B.C., the year in which Hannibal set out with his army on their great march. Hannibal's route, and the later expeditions of Aelius Gallus and Suetonius Paulinus, are also shown, together with Caesar's campaigns.

SCOTLAND

NORTH SEA

BALTIC

ATLANTIC OCEAN

BRITAIN

WALES

ENGLAND

Thames

ENGLISH CHANNEL

lost in A.D. 9

Rhine

Danube

G A U L

A L P S

Col de la
Traversette

Rhône

Massalia

LIGURIAN
SEA

ILLYRIA

L. Trasimeno

PYRENEES

CORSICA

Rome

Cannae

Saguntum

BALEARIC IS.

SARDINIA

Alicante

New Carthage
(Cartagena)

Gades
(Cadiz)

STR. OF GIBRALTAR

Caesarea

M E D I T E R R A

Carthage

SICILY

Zama

GREAT ATLAS

M A U R E T A N I A

N U M I D I A

Ger

3

3

© Geographical Projects

Roman Republic in 218 B.C.
Roman Empire at its greatest extent A.D. 117

Carthage & her colonies 218 B.C.

Hannibal        1  218–202 B.C.

Aelius Gallus    2  25–24 B.C.

Suetonius Paulinus  3  A.D. 42

Julius Caesar's campaigns in Gaul, Spain, Britain & Armenia 61–47 B.C.
Julius Caesar's campaigns in the civil war against Pompey 49–45 B.C.

0    100   200   300   400   500
Miles

Danube

Crimea

CRUCASUS

CASPIAN SEA

BLACK SEA

Cyrus

ARMENIA

Zela

Halys

TAURUS MTS.

Tigris

CYPRUS

CRETE

Euphrates

ANSEA

PERSIAN
GULF

Cleopatris
2

Petra

Arabian

G. OF
SUEZ

Nile

RED SEA

Peninsula

TROPIC OF CANCER

to Marib
2

Turkey and the Halys River (modern Kizil Irmak) in central Turkey. But when Roman troops actually crossed the Taurus Mountains a century later, the military extension of the frontier also involved exploration. Similarly, the invasion of Armenia by the Roman general Lucullus in 69 B.C., and Pompey's advance across the Caucasus into the lands between the Black Sea and the Caspian at about the same period, were more than military expeditions. During both these campaigns, the Roman leaders observed the countries and the peoples they had conquered.

The Romans discovered which was the best pass over the Malyy Caucasus Mountains. They followed and mapped the course of the Cyrus River (now called the Kura). With the aid of a hundred interpreters, they recorded details of the trading methods of 70 tribes on the east coast of the Black Sea. Pompey made notes of trade routes from India which were to be of future use to the Romans. The explorers had a keen eye, too, for the unusual. They noted with amusement that the Armenians used toboggans for getting about on mountain slopes, and even a form of roller skate. This had spiked wooden wheels under the boots to prevent the wearer from slipping.

As the empire grew, the Romans were concerned mainly with securing their frontiers rather than embarking on far-flung campaigns in new lands. An exception was the expedition mounted by the Emperor Augustus in 25 B.C., to penetrate into the largely unknown and unexplored regions of southern Arabia. The aim was to reach Yemen and locate the city of Marib, near present-day San'ā'. From this great ancient capital, some people believed that the Queen of

Left: the Queen of Sheba fording a stream to meet King Solomon. The Bible story of the fabulously rich queen has long captured the imagination of the world, and many legends have grown up around it. This picture, from a prayer book of the 1400's, is based on the legend that Sheba refused to cross a stream by a bridge because she recognized the timbers as those upon which Christ would be crucified. None of the legends say exactly where Sheba's country was situated and several places claim the distinction of being her capital.

Right: a small Roman boat with its crew, from a mosaic found in a villa in Rome.

Above: the town of Marib in Yemen, viewed from the surrounding desert. Some believe it to be the capital of Sheba. In this belief Augustus sent out an expedition under Aelius Gallus to bring it under Roman rule.

Sheba had ruled, 900 years before. From Marib, she was said to have carried fabulous treasure to the court of King Solomon. Yemen was a land of gold, precious stones, myrrh, frankincense, perfumes, spices, and medicinal ointments. For too long, Augustus considered, Arab traders had come north with their caravans. They sold their treasures to Rome and went home rich, having bought nothing in exchange. Augustus resolved that Roman rule and a Roman shipping route would change all that.

In 25 B.C., an expedition under the leadership of Aelius Gallus set out from Cleopatris, a port near present-day Suez. Gallus' orders were to find and conquer the fabulous city of Marib and bring the rich Arabian trade route under Roman control. A force of 10,000 men embarked on the journey aboard 130 specially built ships. Besides Roman legions, the force included Egyptian troops, a contingent of 500 men supplied by King Herod of Judea, and 1,000 Nabataeans from Petra (in what is now Jordan). The Nabataeans were under the command of the Vizier Syllaeus. Gallus' ships sailed southward, keeping close to the Arabian coast. Navigation was difficult, and many of the vessels were wrecked on the coral reefs of the Gulf of Suez. When the men finally landed, about 300 miles down the Arabian coast, Gallus was forced to delay the overland march for many months because of illness among his men.

In the spring of 24 B.C., the 900-mile journey across the barren wastes of the desert of Arabia began. The army made frequent detours in search of wells and precious drinking water. They lived on local grain, dates, and butter. Camels carried only the most essential supplies. The Roman troops clashed with local tribes, but Roman superiority appears to have been overwhelming. The casualty figures read: Arabs killed, 10,000; Romans killed, 2.

During the weary trek south, several towns were captured by the army, but the city that was the main objective of the expedition withstood attack. It is not even certain that the city the Romans besieged was the famous Marib, the Queen of Sheba's capital. Its name is recorded as Mariba, but the reports of the expedition do not state specifically (as they surely would) that this was Sheba's city.

Exhausted by the march and dispirited after their defeat, the soldiers began the return journey. It was beset with difficulties. The explorers spent six hopeless months in the region of Yemen and Hadhramaut in southern Arabia. Misled by local guides, they were often lost in the trackless desert. It was even suggested that Syllaeus, the vizier from Petra, deliberately gave Gallus false directions to prevent the expedition from establishing new routes that would cut Nabataean profits from the trade caravans. It seems more likely, however, that Syllaeus was made the scapegoat for a campaign which had lost a great many men through disease and exhaustion, and was, by Roman standards, a disaster.

Considerably more rewarding and important for exploration were the Roman expeditions to Britain, made by Julius Caesar in 55 and 54 B.C., and by the Emperor Claudius 97 years later. After three

Above: a bust of Julius Caesar. His expedition to Britain in 54 B.C. was far more successful than his first invasion the previous year. In 54 B.C., Caesar landed in what is now Kent, and marched inland, fording the Thames probably above present-day London.

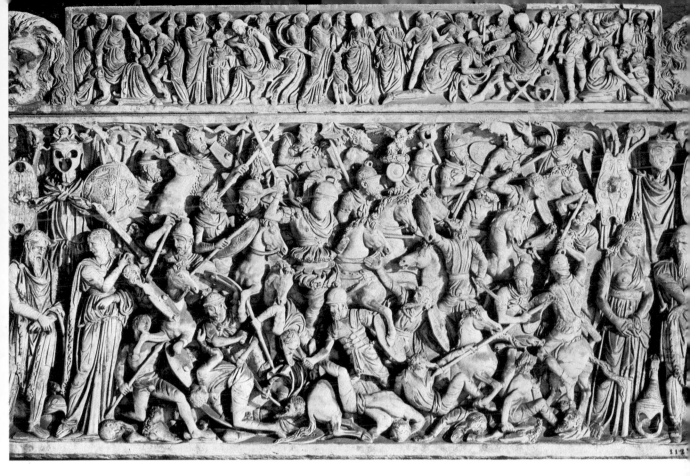

years spent campaigning against the tribes of Gaul (present-day France), Caesar decided to invade the island of Britain. This was a country about which the Romans knew very little. Caesar had probably read that Pytheas the Greek had described Britain as a moist country. He was familiar with the tin trade. And he may also have hoped to find gold in Britain.

In the summer of 55 B.C., Caesar led 2 legions—about 10,000 men—across the English Channel in 80 transports. As the Roman ships approached the coast of Kent in southeast England, the Britons waded into the sea to oppose their landing. A bitter struggle followed, and the Britons were dispersed. The legionaries then made their way inland. But they did not proceed far. The Britons had resorted to guerrilla tactics. Time and again, they poured out of their dense forests and attacked the marching columns of Roman soldiers. The Romans had no cavalry reinforcements. The cavalry transports, which had left Gaul four days after the legions, were driven off shore by bad weather. To make matters worse, Caesar's own ships had been swept off the beach by rising tides, and a violent storm had destroyed many of them. Caesar was forced to give the order to retreat. His expedition lasted only two weeks.

The second invasion of Britain, the following year, was better planned. Caesar chose the month of July to land a force of 30,000 men near Sandwich, in Kent. Marching westward through Kent, he defeated the Britons in a battle near what is now Canterbury. He

Above: Roman soldiers in pitched battle with a Germanic tribe. Julius Caesar showed his brilliant military skill in his campaign to subdue the peoples of Europe, and he brought much of the western part of the continent within the Roman Empire.

Below: a helmet found in Britain of the type worn by Roman soldiers in the 100's. The Romans found the Britons determined adversaries who resorted to guerrilla tactics to defend themselves.

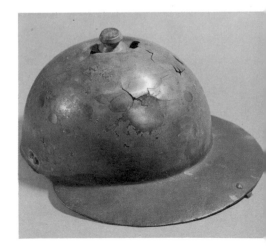

crossed the River Medway and then followed the River Thames, which he forded probably somewhere above present-day London. Leaving the Thames, he continued northward as far as Wheathampstead, near St. Albans (about 20 miles northwest of London). But after spending three months in Britain, Caesar learned that the Gauls were planning a rebellion against Rome. He made an uneasy peace with the Britons, and set sail again for Gaul.

By the time Caesar left Britain, he had formed a picture of the country and its people. Britain was thickly populated, he reported, and the people kept large numbers of cattle. The Britons lived in well-built homesteads and used gold coins or iron bars as money. Hares, fowl, and geese were reared "for pleasure and amusement," and it was considered unlawful to eat them. The climate was less cold than that of Gaul. Caesar had heard that Britain had a month of perpetual darkness, but, not surprisingly, could not confirm this.

Describing the people of the interior, Caesar noted that they did not grow corn, but lived on milk and meat, and clothed themselves with skins. "All the Britons dye their body with woad, which produces a blue color and gives them a terrible appearance in battle," Caesar wrote. "They wear their hair long, and shave the whole of their bodies except the head and upper lip."

Caesar's comments were based on hearsay as well as personal observation, and his facts do not always appear to be accurate. For example, grain is believed to have been widely cultivated in the interior of Britain, and the people used woven material for clothing. Caesar was, however, able to correct Pytheas' estimate of the size of Britain. He recorded that the south coast measured 475 miles, the west coast 665 miles, and the east coast 760 miles.

Claudius' expedition in A.D. 43 had the effect of speeding the growth of Britain as a trading center. His army conquered much of southern Britain and established a camp on the site of London as an advance base for the conquest of the entire island. Within 20 years, London had developed into a fortified town, and was crowded with merchants who came from all over Europe to buy British wares. Between A.D. 70 and 80, Romano-British civilization began in earnest under the Roman general Agricola, who conquered northern

Left: a detail showing a native Briton, from a mosaic floor of a Roman villa in what is now Somerset, in England.

Right: Hadrian's Wall, winding its way across the north of England. It was built at the command of the Emperor Hadrian at the northernmost limit of the territory under Roman control. The wall was to keep the still-unconquered Picts and Scots from invading England.

Left: after Carthage was defeated, Rome took over North Africa and established several Roman provinces there. These ruins are at Djemila, Algeria. Behind the columns can be seen the triumphal arch of the Emperor Nerva.

Below: a mosaic from Rome showing an imaginative picture of life on the Nile. The scene shows the people, the buildings, and local animals such as the hippopotamuses on the riverbanks.

England and North Wales and explored the coast of Scotland. The results of Roman occupation can still be seen all over Britain today, from the remains of forts and towns to the 70-mile-long wall across northern Britain built by the Emperor Hadrian in the A.D. 120's. Thousands of miles of straight Roman roads still exist to show another civil outcome of military exploration.

In Africa, at the other extreme of the Roman Empire, exploration took the Romans across the Grand Atlas mountains, on a search for the source of the River Nile, and probably into Kenya. North Africa had been annexed after the fall of Carthage, and Numidia (now part of eastern Algeria), and Mauretania (now in the northern parts of Morocco and Algeria) became Roman provinces after 46 B.C. Expeditions of Roman cavalry, mounted on fine Numidian horses, rode deep into the African interior south of Caesarea (Cherchel, on the Algerian coast). They brought back elephants, lions, leopards, and bears, which were shipped to Rome. There, the animals were used in one of the most popular entertainments of ancient Rome— fights between men and wild beasts. As many as 5,000 wild animals a day were required for these bloody spectacles in the Colosseum at Rome.

In Mauretania, the Roman consul Suetonius Paulinus became the first European to cross the Atlas mountains. In A.D. 42, he took an expedition 300 miles south from the Mediterranean coast to the mountains. He reported that the peaks were covered with snow even in summer. Ten days' journey took him through a pass to the River Ger (probably what is now the Wadi Guir) and "across deserts covered with black dust occasionally broken by projections of rock that looked as though they had been burned, a region rendered uninhabitable by heat." Where Suetonius crossed is uncertain, but the most likely route would have been between the peaks of the Grand Atlas to the west and the lower Saharan Atlas to the east.

Nineteen years later, in A.D. 61, the Emperor Nero ordered a journey of exploration to seek the source of the River Nile. The mysterious upper reaches of this great river had fascinated the people of the ancient world for centuries. The Egyptians themselves had never traveled farther up the Nile than Khartoum (in present-day Sudan). The Persians, under Cambyses, in 525 B.C., undertook an expedition up the river during which many men died from starvation. Herodotus recorded his journey to the First Cataract at Aswan in 460 B.C., and the Greeks in Egypt had many theories about the sources of the Nile. But in Nero's time the mystery was still unsolved.

Possibly exploration was not the only reason for Nero's expedition. It may have been a reconnaissance in preparation for a campaign against Ethiopia. But whether Nero had military intentions or not, this undertaking developed into an important journey of discovery. The small party of explorers, under the command of two *centurions* (commanders of a *century*, a group of about 100 men), pressed farther south than ever before in their attempt to reach the Nile's source.

The centurions probably followed a caravan route as far as the

Above: two Roman soldiers. It was men like these who tramped the long miles to the outermost edges of the world as it was then known. Much of the Roman expansion was in known countries, but in some of their military expeditions the Roman troops traveled right into the unknown.

Above: Murchison Falls in what is now Uganda. The centurions of the Emperor Nero's expedition reported seeing "a great force of water" gushing from two rocks. Exactly which waterfall they saw has never been discovered.

Dunqulah bend of the Nile in present-day Sudan. During this part of the journey, they found many abandoned Ethiopian towns on the banks of the river. They saw parakeets and dog-faced baboons, and noticed traces of elephants and rhinoceroses. To save time, and to avoid following the Dunqulah bend, they then probably cut across the desert to join the river again at a point just below where Khartoum now stands.

Still they pushed on until, they wrote, "we came to immense

marshes, the outcome of which neither the inhabitants knew nor anyone hopes to know. . . ." Progress on foot was impossible. And even the smallest of boats could not get far amid the thick tangle of weeds that choked the river. In this swampy region, the explorers saw "two rocks from which a great force of river water came falling." The Romans may have taken this to be the source of the Nile itself, but the Roman philosopher Seneca, who reported his conversation with the centurions after their return, wisely did not jump to that conclusion. It seems clear that the explorers had encountered the *sudd*—a mass of floating vegetable matter which can prevent boats sailing up the White Nile. Modern travelers have been unable to identify the two rocks and the great waterfall.

The discovery of the true sources of the Nile is claimed to have been made sometime between A.D. 60 and 70 by a Greek merchant named Diogenes. According to his story, he was sailing on the Indian route down the east coast of Africa when his ship was blown off course as far as what is now Dar es Salaam in Tanzania. Thence he traveled by an unidentified inland route until he "came in 25 days to the lake from which the Nile flows." Reporting Diogenes' discovery, the geographer Ptolemy states that Diogenes reached a place "where the Nile River becomes one from the union of rivers which flow from two lakes." He also mentions that these lakes were located at the extreme limits of a range called the Mountains of the Moon. These mountains, he adds, stretched 500 miles from east to west and were capped with snow, which melted into the lakes.

Ptolemy's account could mean that Diogenes reached the Victoria and Albert lakes. But the mountains that he saw are less easy to identify. There is no mountain range just south of these lakes where Ptolemy situates it. The name Mountains of the Moon is now applied to the Ruwenzori range, discovered by Henry Morton Stanley in 1889. But these mountains, which are frequently obscured by cloud, lie about 200 miles northwest of Lake Victoria and stretch from north to south, not east to west. It seems unlikely that Diogenes traveled as far as the Ruwenzori, although he may have been told about them. Possibly he passed near Mount Kilimanjaro during his journey inland and mistook its twin summits for a range of mountains, although he would have been wrong in thinking that snow from these peaks melted directly into lakes Victoria and Albert. Unfortunately, it is uncertain whether Diogenes saw these lakes and mountains personally. He may have relied on informants, and, indeed, some experts have doubted whether he can be believed at all.

But although the geographic details of Diogenes' story do not fit in exactly with modern knowledge, Ptolemy must have had information on which to base his report. His map of the area is too near the truth to be wholly fabricated. The ultimate source of the Nile lies to the south of the Ruwenzori range, but melted snow from these mountains does flow into the Nile through Lake Albert. It was another 1,700 years, however, before anyone discovered how nearly right Ptolemy had been.

Above: a map of eastern Africa, drawn in the 1400's. This map still shows Ptolemy's Mountains of the Moon as the source of the River Nile. According to Ptolemy, the Greek merchant Diogenes was the first man to reach the mountains. Diogenes' report of his journey does not tally exactly with what is known today about the geography of Africa, and no one knows whether he saw what he reported, or whether he based his account on hearsay.

# The Silk Road from China
# 10

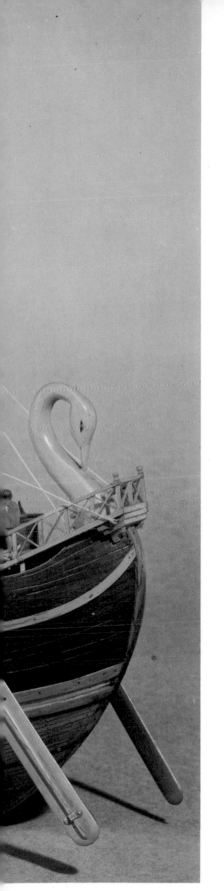

During the 2,000 years in which Western culture was developing around the Mediterranean, another civilization was emerging on the other side of the world. This was the great Chinese Empire. Neither people knew much about the other's existence. Massive mountain ranges, the wide plateaus of Mongolia, and the barren Gobi Desert separated the early civilizations of East and West. The two cultures took shape independently, but shared many of the same basic ways of living which grew out of similar needs.

According to legend, there was civilization in China several thousand years before the birth of Christ. Around 1500 B.C., the earliest culture of which there is archaeological evidence arose in the valley of the Hwang Ho. This was the Shang dynasty. The Shangs were an agricultural people whose capital lay 300 miles south of present-day Peking. Like the Egyptians, the Shangs developed a form of writing which used drawings to represent words. Like the Greeks, they possessed books. Like the Carthaginians, they practiced human sacrifice. Like the Romans, they laid out their cities according to a regular plan. They evolved a system of rule consisting of king, government, and priests. Like most

Left: a model of a Roman merchant ship of the A.D. 100's. These ships carried Roman goods to the ports of Egypt and the Middle East, and returned to Ostia laden with treasures from the East. Although silk was highly prized and very expensive, the Romans did not attempt to voyage to China for it.

Right: a Roman glass jug. Roman glass was one of the commodities exported to the East in exchange for silk.

Above: a ceremonial Chinese bronze axhead, from the Shang period. The Shang dynasty is the first of which there is archaeological evidence.

Right: Ostia, the port of Rome. Ships from all parts of the Roman Empire brought their goods to this port.

ancient peoples, they indulged in a limited form of polygamy—the practice of marrying more than one husband or wife.

As their civilization developed, the Shangs forged bronze swords, built chariots, bred horses, and used stirrups to support their feet when riding. Ruling from their capital, the Great City Shang (present-day An-yang), the Shangs laid the foundations of the powerful nation of China. Under their successors, China began to expand. By 250 B.C., its frontiers stretched eastward to the China Sea and southward as far as the Yangtze River. Later in the 200's B.C., the Emperor Shih Huang Ti, a ruler of the Ch'in dynasty (221 B.C.–207 B.C.), built the Great Wall of China to protect the country's northern frontier from invaders from the rest of Asia.

Right: one of the mosaics found at Ostia. It shows the emblem of a shipping company, presumably based at Ostia when trade there was at its height.

132

The wall, which extends from present-day Lin-yu on the east coast to Kansu province in north central China, is over 1,500 miles long and about 25 feet high. It is believed to have been built by linking shorter walls that were already in existence. By the time of Shih Huang Ti, the Chinese had also set up an elaborate system of roads throughout their country.

China possessed a unique and precious commodity—silk. For centuries this was to be its most valuable export. Silk became one of the most fashionable and highly prized luxuries of the Mediterranean world, and it was by a silken thread that East and West were drawn together. To sell their profitable material, the Chinese needed to find routes to the West. Thus the silk trade opened the way for the exploration of vast areas of little known and hostile lands.

It might have been expected that the Romans would have found their way to the Far East. But no Roman of any consequence is known to have reached China until the A.D. 100's, and by that time the Chinese Silk Road had been established for over 200 years. Although they were forced to pay very high prices for the silk that they imported from China, the Romans appear to have been content to let the Chinese, the Parthians (inhabitants of a kingdom southeast of the Caspian Sea), and the Arabs act as their carriers. The Romans themselves were mainly concerned with bringing to Ostia, the port of Rome, those luxuries that could be obtained within the boundaries of the empire or at least no farther afield than India.

The Romans brought amber from Germany, ivory from Africa, and frankincense from Arabia. From Ceylon, they imported the pearls that were much sought after by Roman women. They looked to India for rice, cotton, coarse cloth, and the highly prized pepper from the Malabar Coast. Ships seeking cargoes for Rome followed the monsoon route to the west coast of India, sailed around Cape Comorin (the southernmost tip of India), called at Ceylon, and even ventured north into the Bay of Bengal. But apparently there was not enough incentive to voyage farther still and brave the Strait of Malacca between Malaya and Sumatra to bring back the soft, luxurious material and silk thread from China. Not that foreign traders would have been at all welcome. The Chinese guarded the secret of silk manufacture so successfully that they retained a world monopoly for thousands of years. So great a mystery surrounded the origin of silk that even as late as the 100's B.C. a Roman writer as well informed as Virgil imagined that it grew on trees.

The Chinese themselves have left little information about the early development of silk. An ancient legend tells that silk was discovered in about 2700 B.C. A Chinese empress was asked by her husband to find out what was damaging his mulberry trees. She found what appeared to be white worms eating the leaves and spinning shiny cocoons. When she accidentally dropped one of the cocoons into hot water a fine thread began to unwind. Delicately she unpicked it until she had unraveled 4,400 yards of silk.

Whatever the truth about the discovery of silk, very little of it,

Above: Chinese ladies preparing a length of newly-woven silk. Silk was one of the most sought-after luxuries for the Romans, but the Chinese held a monopoly of its manufacture for more than 3,000 years. This picture is actually painted on silk. It dates from 1082–1135, but is based on an even older work by Chang Hsuan, a court painter active from 713–742. *(Museum of Fine Arts, Boston.)*

either as thread or made up into cloth, was seen outside China until the rise of the Han dynasty in 206 B.C. During the rule of the Hans, the boundaries of China were pushed back until China was as large as the entire Roman Empire. The emperor Wu Ti, who reigned from 141 B.C.–87 B.C., trebled the size of the Chinese Empire. He sent embassies to lands beyond his new frontiers, and this led to the export of silk on a large scale.

In his endless wars against the northern Huns, Wu Ti wanted to make an alliance with the Yue-Chi, a people living a fugitive existence in central Asia. They had been driven west of the Chinese borders, and the emperor probably hoped that they would help the Chinese to establish trade routes. The man he sent on this mission was an officer named Chang Ch'ien, a popular, generous-hearted soldier described as having "strong physique." He needed it. He was to be away from Changan, Wu Ti's capital, for 12 years. He was to travel thousands of miles through unknown lands, and endure great hardships.

Chang's expedition started disastrously. On the enemy's borders he and his party of some 100 men were captured by the Huns. Chang remained a prisoner for 10 years, and then, in about 128 B.C., he escaped with some of his followers and the barbarian woman he had married during his captivity. Chang continued westward and finally found the Yue-Chi, who had settled in Bactria beyond the Pamirs and south of the Oxus River. He stayed with them for some

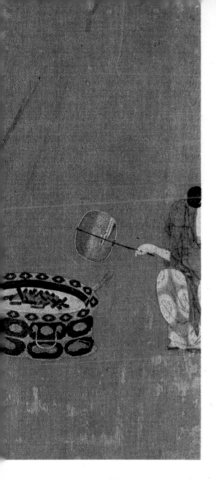

time, but he could not persuade them to become China's allies in the fight against the Huns.

On his return journey to China by way of Tibet, Chang was once again taken prisoner by the enemy, but this time he escaped after only a short time in captivity. Despite the apparent failure of his mission, Chang's arrival home with his wife and the survivors of the expedition was greeted as a triumph by the emperor. Wu Ti considered that Chang had brought back something even more valuable than a military alliance. He had acquired unique information about other tribes and unknown territories. He could advise on the best and safest routes to carry China's trade into Asia Minor and Europe. After a further reconnaissance expedition made by Chang in 105 B.C., the Silk Road to the West was opened.

Within a few years, caravans of mules and camels were following the Silk Road 6,000 miles from northwest China to the Mediterranean Sea. With their cargoes of thread and bales of patterned damasks and taffetas, they set out from Changan westward along the valley of the Hwang Ho (Yellow River). They took the tracks that led north of the mountains of Tibet to Kashgar (near the present-day frontier between western China and southeastern Russia). On this part of the journey they had to choose whether to travel north or south of the burning desert of Taklamakan. The more usual way was to the south, where there was a chain of oases to provide water for men and animals.

Above: the Chinese emperor Wu Ti of the Han dynasty, who sent Chang Ch'ien on a mission to make an alliance with the Yue-Chi. Chang was away from Wu Ti's capital for 12 years. *(Museum of Fine Arts, Boston.)*
Below: a pottery figure of a warrior, which dates from the Han dynasty.

Above: the ramparts of Bactra, capital of the ancient land of Bactria in what is now Afghanistan. The city, which was later renamed Wazirabad, was one of the main centers for the silk trade, and a stopping place on the road between the Pamirs and Merv. In Chang Ch'ien's time, this part of the Silk Road was controlled by the Yue-Chi people.

Right: this map of Asia, Europe, and Africa shows the journeys of both Chang Ch'ien and Hsuan-tsang. It also shows the most important trade routes to China by both sea and land. The Great Wall of China and the boundaries of the early (Western) and later (Eastern) Han dynasties are also shown.

As far as Kashgar, the route lay in Chinese-dominated territory. The next stage of the journey took the caravans over the Pamirs and on, by way of Samarkand or Bactria, to the oasis city of Merv (near the present-day city of Mary on the border between Russia and Iran). Merv was regarded by central Asiatic people as the cradle of mankind. This part of the Silk Road was controlled by the Yue-Chi, the people to whom Chang had been sent by the emperor.

The route was divided into four stages: from Changan to Kashgar; from Kashgar to Merv; from Merv to Ctesiphon (south of what is now Baghdad in Iraq); and from Ctesiphon to the ports of the Mediterranean. Each of these stages was under the control of a different people, and it appears that caravan drivers traveled only a certain distance and then transferred their merchandise to the next driver. Whether these drivers were acting as agents for the original Chinese merchant, or were just carriers, is uncertain. Possibly the Chinese financial interest ended with the first change of hands, and the silk was sold, resold, and sold again in the thriving markets of the key cities along the route.

Whatever the method, it created a series of middlemen, each of whom took a large profit. This forced up the cost of silk, so that by

N

ARCTIC CIRCLE                                                    ARCTIC CIRCLE

Scandinavia

URAL MOUNTAINS

Volga

BALTIC SEA

SHETLAND IS.

ORKNEY IS.

Dnepr

Volga

CASPIAN SEA

PARTHIA

Kyzyl Kum

Mongolia

Gobi Desert

Manchuria

built c.300 B.C.

built c.200 B.C.

Tashkent

Samarkand

TIEN SHAN

Turfan

built 213-1112 B.C.

Oxus

Merv

Bactria

Balkh

PAMIRS

Kashgar

Taklamakan Desert

Shang (An-yang)

Khotan

HINDU KUSH

Peshawar

Hwang Ho

Changan

Kashmir

Indus

EAST CHINA SEA

Multan

Yangtze R.

TROPIC OF CANCER

Indus

Benares

Ganges

PACIFIC OCEAN

ARABIAN SEA

Canton

BAY OF BENGAL

Malabar Coast

Madras

G. OF SIAM

SOUTH CHINA SEA

C. Comorin

CEYLON

STR. OF MALACCA

Malay Pena.

INDIAN OCEAN

EQUATOR

Chang Ch'ien 1 138–126 B.C.

Hsuan-tsang 2 A.D. 629–645

Trade routes

Great Wall of China

Boundary of early (Western) Han dynasty c.100 B.C.

Boundary of later (Eastern) Han dynasty c.A.D.100

250   500   750   1000   1250   1500   Miles

© Geographical Projects

Above: the ruins of Palmyra, lying under the hot desert sun. Palmyra was a meeting place for several caravan routes, and the splendor of what remains shows what a wealthy city it once was. It was built at an oasis in the Syrian Desert and became so important that the Romans developed an elaborate system to guard the routes leading to and from the city.

the time it reached Rome the price was exorbitant. The most serious increase occurred in the third stage of the Silk Road immediately west of Merv in Parthian territory. The Parthians were strong enough to exercise absolute control on all goods passing through their empire. They probably imposed a heavy tax on the caravans which added still further to the eventual price of the silk.

From Merv, it was about 1,300 miles' journey over mountainous territory to the Parthian royal city of Ctesiphon. The final journey to the Mediterranean ports began there. The most direct route would have been due west, reaching the coast at, say, Tyre. This

was, however, impossible as it would have meant a trek of 400 miles through the waterless Syrian Desert which even camels could not manage. Instead, the caravans went northwest, following the fertile valley of the Euphrates River.

Those on the main Silk Road, whose objective was Rome, continued up the river to Zeugma, in present-day Syria. Those whose destinations were the more southerly coastal towns of Syria, Palestine, and Egypt branched off at Hīt on the Euphrates River. They then headed northwest for Palmyra in Syria, skirting the north of the Syrian Desert.

Palmyra, which lies about 130 miles northeast of Damascus, was an oasis village which Rome and the caravan trade transformed into a magnificent and thriving city. Isolated in the middle of the desert, its ruins still testify to its former glory. From Palmyra, the silk went to Damascus and on to textile-manufacturing and dyeing cities such as Tyre and Gaza. Palmyra was also the starting point for a southerly route through Petra (in the southwest of present-day Jordan) to Alexandria, Arabia, and the Red Sea ports. So important was this caravan city that the Romans developed and guarded routes to and from it by building forts and sinking wells every 24 miles along the way. They established an armed camel corps to patrol the route, and the caravans traveled in convoy under its protection. These caravans consisted of as many as 3,000 camels, and the geographer Strabo likened them to armies on the march.

Silk bound for Rome itself had reached the western limit of the Parthian Empire at Zeugma. At this frontier town of the Roman Empire, there was a bridge across the Euphrates. At Antioch (Antakya in southern Turkey), 150 miles farther on, merchandise

Right: the head of a noblewoman from Palmyra. She is richly adorned with jewelry, as befits an aristocratic lady living in one of the wealthiest cities of the Roman Empire. The carving itself, dating from the A.D. 100's, shows how Oriental influences mingled with Greco-Roman styles in the art of the frontier lands.

was loaded on ships for the voyage that completed the journey. By the time the material was on sale in the Vicus Tuscus, Rome's chief silk market, a year had passed since it had left China.

The effort involved in these expeditions might seem excessive, but supply was answering demand. Silk had become the rage of Rome, the symbol of wealth and position, and a necessity for all noblewomen. They delighted in wearing gauzy, semitransparent silk dresses. "I see silken clothes," wrote Seneca, "that in no degree afford protection either to the body or modesty of the wearer, and clad in which no woman could honestly swear she is not naked." Pliny was scandalized at the practice (which grew into an industry on the Aegean island of Kós) of unraveling and reweaving silk yarn into see-through material.

So great a drain was the cost of silk on the Roman treasury that attempts were made first to fix prices and then to restrict the import of silk along with other expensive and exotic goods. This official attitude was probably one of the main reasons why Rome was slow in opening up her own trade routes to China. It was not until the reign of Marcus Aurelius in the A.D. 100's, when war with Parthia caused a complete breakdown in the overland Silk Road, that Roman merchants showed any enterprise. In A.D. 166, some private adventurers succeeded in reaching China by sea, thus establishing the first direct contact between the great empires of East and West. But the sea route to China was long, dangerous, and infested with pirates, and few sailors dared to repeat the voyage. From time to time over the next few centuries Rome sent what are described as "embassies" to China by the sea route. But these visits did nothing to bring down the price of silk, or to establish a regular sea trade with China.

Right: the Vicus Tuscus, the silk market near the Forum at Rome. It was here that the silk imported from China was eventually sold. By that time its price was enormous, forced up by the number of middlemen who had taken their profits as it was brought west.

Marcus Aurelius tried to set an example by not wearing silk, and would not let his wife wear it. But it was the Byzantine Emperor Justinian—ruler of the eastern half of what had been the Roman Empire—who caused the worst crisis by fixing prices in A.D. 540. By this time the Persians (who had overthrown the Parthians) had a virtual monopoly of the silk trade. They refused to sell at the Roman figure. Faced with the possibility of being cut off from all supplies of silk, the Romans resorted to what must be the earliest example of industrial espionage. They decided to smuggle the

secret of silk cultivation out of China and to start producing silk themselves.

The accounts of this audacious undertaking are colorful but may not be true. It is said that, twelve years after Justinian's edict, two monks presented themselves to the emperor in Constantinople, capital of the Byzantine Empire. They belonged to the Nestorian order, long exiled for their heresy in denying Mary as the mother of God. Their proposition to Justinian was also unorthodox.

The monks had traveled from India, where they had lived near the Chinese border. They were able to cross the frontier into China without exciting suspicion and were prepared, they said, to penetrate into the closely guarded silk-producing area, steal some silkworms' eggs, and smuggle them out. It was a dangerous mission. Death was their certain fate if they were caught. They would need to be well paid.

Cost was unimportant compared with the chance of starting silk

production in the Roman world. Justinian promised the monks a suitable reward, and they traveled back to the East. Many months went by. Then, at last, the two Nestorians presented themselves once again to the emperor. They had with them the precious eggs, which they had hidden in the hollow of bamboo canes. It is a peculiar feature of such stories that, vague though they are in outline, they are surprisingly minute in odd details. The names and particulars of the monks are completely unknown, and yet we are told the exact number of stolen eggs—550.

From these eggs, hatched and reared on the mulberry trees of Constantinople, grew the silkworms that freed the West from reliance on China. After more than 3,000 years, during which China had so carefully guarded its secret, silk could be produced in the West. Syria became the center for silk production, and by the end of the A.D. 500's was apparently able to meet all the demands for silk in the Mediterranean world.

Above: Nestorian priests. It is said that two Nestorian monks eventually solved the mystery of how silk was made, smuggling silkworm eggs out of China in bamboo canes. At last, the Chinese monopoly was broken and the Romans could make silk themselves.

# The End of the Beginning

# 11

The fall of Rome in A.D. 476 left no nation to carry on voyages and land expeditions on a large scale. Barbarian invaders from the north and east swept into the western part of the Roman Empire, replacing the Roman provinces with a confusion of small, individual kingdoms which were constantly at war with one another. Although the eastern part of the empire, centered on Constantinople, survived, it was fully occupied with defending, rather than expanding, its frontiers. In China, the Han dynasty had fallen, and the Chinese Empire had split into a collection of small states. The known world was in a turmoil of wars, migrations, and violent political change. Trade, which had been one of the prime motives for exploration,

Left: a Roman road map. The Romans built magnificent roads, many of which have survived to this day. As mapmakers, however, they were less expert. This map, a copy made in the 1200's of a Roman map of the 200's, does not attempt to show the true size, shape, or position of the various features it depicts. All the rivers appear to run from east to west, regardless of their real course—the Rhine, for instance, actually flows south to north.

Above: a coin showing the head of Attila the Hun, leader of one of the barbarian tribes that invaded the Roman Empire in its dying years.

came to a halt as a series of small, self-sufficient communities developed where once great civilizations had flourished.

During this period of upheaval, the urge to travel was kept alive to some extent by a new force—religion. The missionaries of Christianity—the religion adopted by the Roman Empire in its last days of power—went forth to seek converts in new lands. And as early as the A.D. 300's, small parties of Christian pilgrims traveled to Jerusalem from the farthest corners of the known world. Although these pilgrims were not explorers, their journeys were very ambitious undertakings for their time.

In China, too, religion provided an incentive for travel. A number

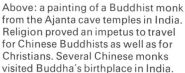
Above: a painting of a Buddhist monk from the Ajanta cave temples in India. Religion proved an impetus to travel for Chinese Buddhists as well as for Christians. Several Chinese monks visited Buddha's birthplace in India.

of Chinese converts to Buddhism, which had been brought to China by A.D. 100, made the journey to India to visit the birthplace of Buddha and seek greater understanding of the beliefs of the Buddhist religion. One such traveler was the Chinese monk Fa-Hsien, who set out from Changan in about A.D. 400 with three companions. After six years' journey, the four men reached central India. There they spent a further six years studying and traveling in India and Ceylon before returning to China by sea.

In the A.D. 600's, another fervent Chinese Buddhist made a vow to "travel in the countries of the west in order to question the wise men on the points that were troubling his mind." His name was Hsuan-tsang, and he was one of the greatest travelers of the ancient world. By the time of Hsuan-tsang, China had been reunited under the Sui dynasty, which, in 618, had been succeeded by the T'angs. Central Asia was still in a state of turmoil, and the emperor forbade Hsuan-tsang to leave China. Undeterred, the 19-year-old Hsuan set out to cross the desert wastes of the Gobi. Abandoned by his guide and by his friends, he found his way by following the tracks of camels and other pack animals. At one stage he went without water for five days after dropping his waterskin. But he finally reached Turfan in western China, where a local ruler provided him with an escort of men to accompany him on the next stage of his journey, and pack animals to carry his belongings.

With his new companions, Hsuan fought his way across the icy Tien Shan mountains. In the course of this crossing, 13 men and many of the animals lost their lives. But still Hsuan traveled on. He reached Tashkent and pushed on to Samarkand. His journey took him over the Oxus River and into Bactria, where he visited a number of Buddhist monasteries. Then he crossed the Hindu Kush, traveled through the Khyber Pass to Peshāwar (in what is now the northern part of West Pakistan), and explored the Swat Valley. Before him lay the gorges of the Indus, where, he wrote, "the roads were very dangerous. . . . Sometimes one had to cross on rope bridges, sometimes by clinging to chains. Now there were gangways hanging in midair, now flying bridges flung across precipices." These hazards once behind him, Hsuan reached Kashmir, on the northern borders of India. He remained there for two years, studying under the guidance of a learned Buddhist monk.

In 633, Hsuan traveled to the sacred Ganges River and spent several years visiting cities, monasteries, and libraries. He then journeyed southward across the Deccan and northward along the west coast of the Bay of Bengal. After exploring the region of Assam in northeastern India, he at last decided to set out for home. He made his way back across the Punjab and traveled up the valley of the Oxus River. In the face of biting winds, he journeyed over the Pamirs and made his way down to Kashgar. He then followed the route of the silk caravans to Khotan and across the desert of Taklamakan. In 645, 16 years after leaving China against the emperor's orders, he returned in triumph to his native land. At the emperor's request, he wrote a detailed account of his long and arduous journey, which included a great deal of valuable information about the lands he had passed through. Hsuan then spent the rest of his life translating the 740 religious manuscripts he had brought back with him from India.

Apart from the peaceful journeys of Hsuan-tsang and pilgrims like him, religion also inspired wars of conquest. The end of the Roman Empire left the Mediterranean world divided and vulnerable. Swiftly, ruthlessly, and with astonishing efficiency, the Arabs swept to power. Inspired by the teachings of the prophet Mohammed (born in Mecca in about A.D. 570), they surged north into Syria and made Damascus their capital. Then they spread east and west.

Above: Hsuan-tsang, the young Chinese Buddhist who traveled to India in the 600's to learn more about his faith. His arduous journey lasted 16 years. Some of this time he spent in India studying in various monasteries.

147

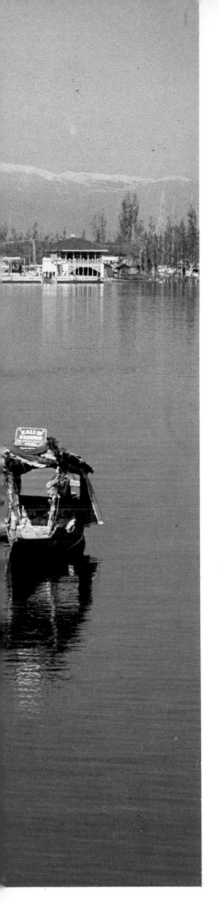

In Persia, they won immediate victory, and they proceeded to carry their religious beliefs as far as the Indus. A new capital was set up at Baghdad. The forces of Islam—the religion of Mohammed's followers —also drove westward to conquer Egypt and Libya. The Moslem Arabs, superbly mounted and armed with deadly bows and arrows, streamed along the north coast of Africa to the Pillars of Hercules, which they named Gebel-at-Tarik—Gibraltar. The capture of Alexandria gave them a great port from which to attack and capture Crete and Cyprus. Spain fell to them, and they established a frontier along the Pyrenees. Within 100 years, the Moslem Empire stretched from northern Spain to India. Trade was revived, and the Arabs made regular voyages to the East.

But while the travelers of the Far East and the conquerors of the Moslem world kept the spirit of exploration alive, most of the inhabitants of Europe felt little urge to challenge the unknown. Hardly any journeys of exploration were made from the Western world during the first 700 years after the birth of Christ. The Europeans of the time lived in an enclosed world, bounded by the Atlantic Ocean to the west and the vast plains of Asia to the east. Fear and superstition prevented them from venturing beyond the world they knew. An immense change in the attitudes and beliefs of the peoples of Europe was needed to generate the excitement and overwhelming curiosity that inspired the great explorers.

Is it true that no sailor had been out into the Atlantic farther

Left: one of the lakes in Kashmir, with the mountains in the background. Hsuan-tsang spent two years in Kashmir—a region on the northern borders of India—studying with a learned Buddhist monk there.

Below: a manuscript illustration of two Moors in Spain, playing a form of chess. The tide of Islam swept north throughout what is now Spain, and the Moorish rule was maintained in parts of the peninsula for over 700 years.

west than the Canary Islands by A.D. 700? There is speculation, notably promoted by the Norwegian ethnologist Thor Heyerdahl, that by this time the Egyptians may have reached the New World— the Americas—in boats made of papyrus, a type of water reed. Heyerdahl does not, however, venture a definite date. It has also been suggested that the Phoenicians and the Chinese may have sailed to the shores of America in early times. There is even an idea (based on an inscription found on a stone in Tennessee in 1885) that Jews reached North America sometime before 500 B.C. But little real evidence in support of these suggestions has ever been found.

Disunity, warfare, and the decline in trade, all played their part in discouraging exploration in the West during the Dark Ages—the period between the A.D. 400's and 900's. But there was yet another force behind this prolonged lack of interest in foreign lands—the church. Although the rise of Christianity led to a limited amount of travel, the church also played a decisive part in blocking the progress of geographical knowledge. Hostile to pagan learning and achievement, the Christianized Roman Empire, centered in Constantinople, was satisfied with the limits set on the world by the Bible. The scientific theories of the great Greek philosophers,

Above: Thor Heyerdahl's primitive craft, *Ra II,* in which he crossed the Atlantic in an effort to prove that it would have been possible for the Egyptians to reach America in papyrus boats. He speculates that they may have built the pyramids found in Mexico.

astronomers, and geographers were denounced as heretical—contrary to accepted belief.

The church enclosed the world in blinkers. It even rejected the knowledge, by then fully accepted by all men of learning, that the world was a sphere. God had created the universe, the churchmen believed, and it was undesirable to pursue knowledge that added to, and might run contrary to, Holy Scripture. This attitude is exemplified in a book called *Christian Topography,* written by Cosmas, a monk who was born in Alexandria in the A.D. 500's. Cosmas attempted to disprove the ideas of men such as the Greek geographer and astronomer Eratosthenes, who believed the world to be a sphere, and who, as early as 200 B.C., had calculated its circumference with remarkable accuracy. Turning to the Bible for guidance, Cosmas found a phrase comparing the world to the Tabernacle of Moses. The Tabernacle, a place of worship built by Moses and the Israelites at the command of God, was a large, rectangular tent. Cosmas therefore represented the universe as a rectangular box with the sky as its curved "lid." In the box, he believed, lay the inhabited part of the world, which was surrounded by ocean. Beyond the lid of the box lay heaven.

As well as stifling exploration, this lopsided theology had a

Below: a drawing from Cosmas' *Christian Topography*, showing Cosmas' view of the world. Basing his idea on a phrase in the Bible, he pictured it in the form of the Tabernacle of Moses. The walls and lid form the heavens and the sun rises and sets over the center mountain, while from above the Creator surveys his handiwork.

serious effect on geography. In the place of maps with scientific value, monks began to produce *wheel maps*. These showed Jerusalem as the center of a flattened, circular world. The chief divisions of land and sea radiated from the hub of Jerusalem like spokes. Piety also demanded that the sacred east, and not north, should be placed at the top of the map. As a result, no map of any geographical value was produced for nearly a thousand years. So great was the effect of the church's determination to ignore scientific fact that as the centuries passed many of the discoveries of the ancient world were forgotten. Europeans began to regard the church's theories as fact, and a web of fear and superstition grew up about the world beyond Europe. Nowhere was this more apparent than in the prevailing belief during the Dark Ages that the world was indeed flat, and that, if a sailor voyaged too far, he would fall off the edge.

Throughout the Middle Ages, the only real map of the world to which men could refer was the one devised by Claudius Ptolemy in about A.D. 150. Ptolemy, a Greek, was the greatest geographer and astronomer of ancient times. Although his idea of the world was limited and not strictly accurate, it was the most complete view available, and comparatively little information was added to it until the end of the 1400's. Ptolemy's map may therefore be regarded as a

Below: in his book, written between 535 and 547, Cosmas rejected the idea that the earth was round. He found the idea of a world facing downward, and men walking about beneath our feet, ridiculous, and argued that, according to the Bible, there was only one "face of the earth" which God gave to man for him to dwell upon.

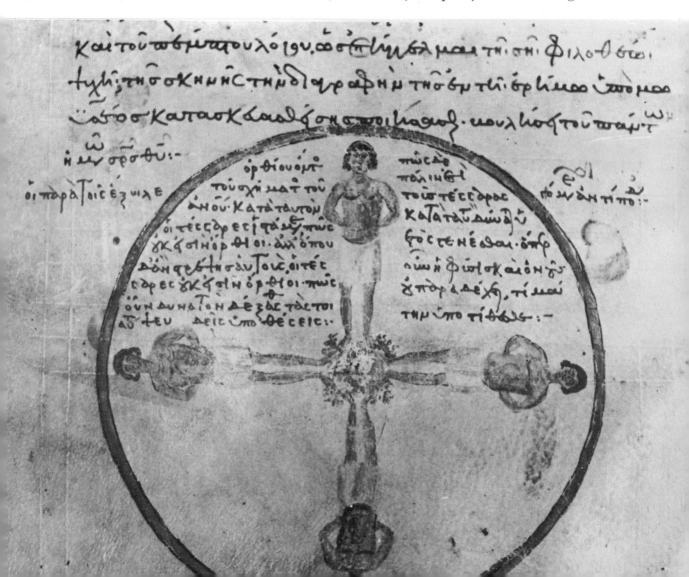

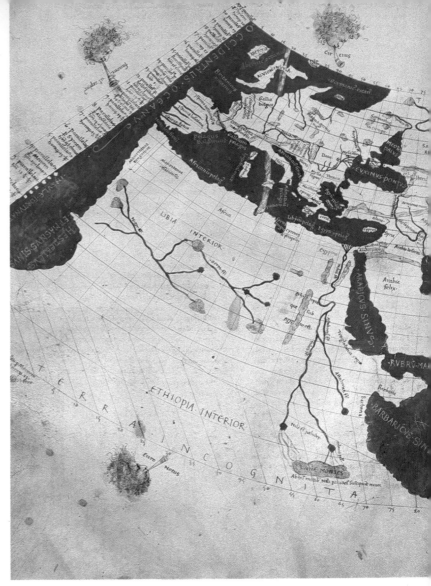

Above: a doorway of the cathedral in Florence, Italy, depicting the great geographer Ptolemy, who lived and worked in Alexandria in the A.D. 100's.

fair representation of the world as it was known in A.D. 700.

The curious thing about Ptolemy's map is that, strictly speaking, it does not exist. Ptolemy himself may never have drawn more than rough sketches of his ideas for his own use. But he did prepare a volume of instruction in mapmaking which was used as a guide by later cartographers. The representations which are today referred to as "Ptolemy's map" are based directly on these instructions, or are copied from earlier versions of Ptolemy's ideas. The oldest of these still in existence dates only from the A.D. 1200's, more than a thousand years after Ptolemy wrote his book.

Fortunately, Ptolemy's *Geography*—also called *Instruction in Mapdrawing*—contained the sum total of all geographical knowledge up to his time. He provided the names of 8,000 places, and the lines of latitude on which they were to be found. For 180 of these places he also gave the lines of longitude. Like every geographer of ancient times, Ptolemy had to be content to show only half the world, extending from China in the east to Africa in the west through 180°

Left: one of the world maps based on the theories of Ptolemy, the greatest geographer of the ancient world. This map was drawn in the 1400's, when Ptolemy's *Geography* (written in about A.D. 150) was still the chief source of reference for geographers. Like the Greek philosopher Aristotle, Ptolemy believed the Indian Ocean to be an inland sea, and thought that an unknown land in the south linked Africa with eastern Asia. He represented Asia as stretching indefinitely away to the east—a view which later influenced Columbus in the belief that he could reach Asia after only a short voyage across the Atlantic.

of longitude. His latitude extended to 67° north of the equator, and to 16° south of it. The lines of longitude and latitude are curved as they should be, and Ptolemy's world has the appearance of an inverted fan with the lines of longitude as ribs. The ribs do not converge at the North Pole, for Ptolemy did not know of the Arctic or attempt to map it. To the south of the equator his *projection* —the depiction on a flat surface of what is really a sphere—turns sharply downward at the edge of the fan. This was a conventional device, and saved putting in the lower part of the globe about which he was also ignorant.

The one serious mistake made by Ptolemy lies in enclosing the Indian Ocean by a southern land mass. This means that Ptolemy did not accept Herodotus' account of the Phoenicians' journey around Africa. He joined East Africa just south of the equator to China, showing the Indian Ocean as a vast inland sea. This was a misconception that was to persist until Bartholomeu Dias rounded the Cape of Good Hope in the 1400's.

Another strange feature of the map is the way in which the Indian Peninsula is shrunk and Ceylon increased to 14 times its real size. This is particularly surprising because a Greek doctor of the 500's B.C. had written a book on India, and the Romans had visited Ceylon. In addition, a travel manual called the *Periplus of the Erythrean Sea*, written by an unknown Greek seaman in about 30 B.C., gave a detailed description of the Indian coastline, as well as describing the Red Sea ports and the East African coast. However, both the Indus and the Ganges rivers are correctly placed on Ptolemy's map, the first thanks to the information brought back by Alexander, the second probably from data in the *Periplus*.

The Malay Peninsula and Indochina—or possibly Burma—are indicated a trifle sketchily. Until Nero's time, the Greeks and Romans thought of Burma as an island. Then they discovered it to be a great headland which they called Chryse. Ptolemy turns his land mass south after what he calls the "Great Gulf," which may be the Gulf of Siam, or possibly the South China Sea, of which he would have heard from returning traders.

The eastern limit of the map fades out into *Terra Incognita*— unknown land—as it was to remain until the expedition of Marco Polo late in the A.D. 1200's. But because of the Silk Road, central Asia could be mapped with some accuracy. The Caspian Sea had been explored by the Greeks as a result of expeditions they had made into the Ural Mountains in search of gold and fur. Scythia, too, was known through Greek traders who had gone north of the

Left: an example of Byzantine silk. Even after the collapse of the Roman Empire, Eastern goods were still traded along the traditional Silk Road.

Black Sea into southern Russia for metals, ceramics, wheat, and gold. Information about the Ukraine was plentiful. Herodotus had visited Olbia, a colony near the Dnepr estuary in western Russia. Strabo, too, had traveled to the Dnepr River and reported that it was navigable for 70 miles. Under the Emperor Hadrian, a trade route had been established by the Romans as far north as Kiev.

Neither Norway nor the Baltic Sea appear on Ptolemy's map. For the far north there was only Pytheas' description of Thule to go on, and, when the Romans recalled their northern armies from the Rhine in A.D. 16, Scandinavia had still not been explored. The oddly shaped British Isles must have been far better known than the map suggests. After over 100 years of Roman occupation, Britain must have been fully surveyed. The Orkney Islands, the Shetland Islands, and the Hebrides off the coast of Scotland were on maps before the time of Agricola, the Roman general whose fleet had explored the coasts of Scotland and may even have sailed around Britain in about A.D. 80. Ireland, too, should have been more accurately depicted by Ptolemy. Although the interior was not

Above: the map of the British Isles from the manuscript of Agathodaemon. It is odd that Ptolemy did not have more accurate information on the shape of the islands, for they must have been surveyed during the years of Roman occupation.

explored for many centuries, the coast, including the town of Eblana (on the site of present-day Dublin), had been described by the Roman geographer Pomponius Mela in A.D. 43.

Continuing south past Spain to the west coast of Africa, little more is shown on the map than had been revealed by Hanno's colonizing expedition more than 400 years before the birth of Christ. South of the equator, Ptolemy lets the continent trail away vaguely. But the east coast of Africa must have been better known than the map indicates, for information about it had been included in the *Periplus*. However, the reluctance of Arab sailors to venture much below the equator accounts for many misconceptions, not all of

Above: Pico de Teide, Tenerife, in the Canary Islands. The Phoenicians and the Greeks certainly knew of the islands' existence. The Greeks said that this mountain, which they called Mount Atlas, supported the sky.

Right: pottery from Las Palmas, in the Canaries. It has been suggested that the original inhabitants of the islands might have been of Egyptian origin.

them geographical. The Arabs are said to have thought that the southern seas boiled, just as the Portuguese later believed a similar legend about the sea to the south of Cape Bojador on the coast of present-day Spanish Sahara.

The Azores were not mapped in A.D. 700, even though they may have been visited by the Carthaginian sailor Himilco. But Hanno had probably visited Madeira, and the Canary Islands were also known at this time. The Roman historian Pliny, who was writing in the A.D. 100's, knew of five islands and described Tenerife and La Palma. Ptolemy mentions six and names three, though he sites them too far out in the Atlantic.

Most of the rivers which caused so much curiosity among early peoples had been explored by Ptolemy's time. He knew of the Volga and described it as flowing into the Caspian Sea. Tiberius (who became Roman emperor at the time of Christ) had followed the Danube to its source, and Roman explorers had navigated most of the main rivers of middle Europe to open up southern Germany. Sources of rivers were of the greatest fascination, and, presumably trusting the story of Diogenes, Ptolemy shows the Nile rising in the Mountains of the Moon.

As the ancient world came to an end and Europe entered the Middle Ages, not all of the ideas and achievements of the early civilizations were forgotten. But it was in the Moslem Empire, above all, that the great heritage of classical learning was preserved. The Moslems collected many texts in Damascus, and later in Baghdad, where a scientific academy was opened for translation into Arabic. Ptolemy's *Geography* was just one of the numerous works that appeared in an Arabic version and served an Arab author as a model for his own book on geography. Hundreds of years later, at the time of the Renaissance (the great revival of learning which began in Europe in the 1300's), the Arabic versions of the ancient classical works were discovered in the universities the Moslems had founded in Spain, and the libraries of the Arab world. Now they could be translated into Latin—the language of most educated

Below: an Arab map of Ceylon. Drawn in the 1000's, it accompanies a manuscript by the Arab geographer Musa al-Khawarizmi, who was strongly influenced by Ptolemy.

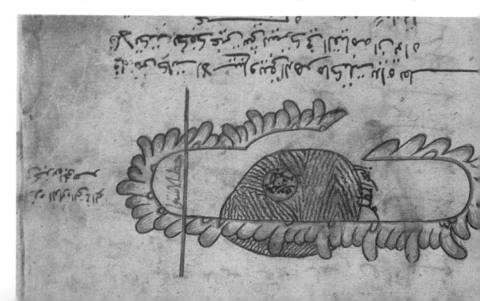

Below: the world map of al-Idrisi, 1154. Arab maps of this period were drawn with the south at the top, and the Indian Ocean is therefore shown above the Mediterranean Sea. According to al-Idrisi, the world was flat and measured 22,900 miles around the edge. He believed that it was encircled by water which held it "stable in space like the yolk of an egg." (Bodleian Library, Oxford. MS. Pococke. 375, fols. 3v–4r.)

Europeans in the Middle Ages and of most books of the time.

When the work of Ptolemy was translated into Latin soon after its rediscovery in A.D. 1407, it became a major influence in the renewal of interest in geography and on plans for the voyages that were to launch the great age of discovery in the 1400's. But hundreds of years before these voyages had even been dreamed of, two peoples were to take up the challenge of the unknown. From Ireland, and from the misty regions of the north, the Irish and Vikings would strike out across the Atlantic for new lands beyond the horizon.

# Appendix

Above: a Roman soldier, perhaps one of those who marched to the farthest reaches of the then known world.

Man's first uncertain steps into the unknown were made long before recorded times. And the earliest references to exploration, dating from about 2500 B.C., are tantalizingly incomplete. No travelers' diaries or ships' logs have come down to give us firsthand accounts of these daring expeditions. The story of the first explorers begins with records chiseled in stone and bronze, and painted on the walls of temples and tombs. Other accounts are derived from ancient legends that were passed on by word of mouth from one generation to the next.

Most of our knowledge of early exploration comes from sources which are hundreds of years later than the actual events. History—that is, the written record of man's achievements—did not exist much before the 400's B.C. It was at this time that Herodotus, who came to be called "The Father of History," wrote the nine books that make up his *Histories*. These books, which have survived from antiquity, are packed with lively details about the lands that Herodotus visited during his extensive travels. And they contain a great deal of valuable information about the first explorers.

From the time of Herodotus, books were written on papyrus, a perishable material, and no complete specimens survive from the classical period. The best we can hope for are copies of an original or, more likely, copies of copies. In the centuries before the invention of printing, dozens—perhaps even hundreds—of transcribers have come between us and the original document. With each new transcription or translation, errors (or even deliberate alterations) may have crept in. But without the invaluable records that have come down to us by this long and devious route, the history of the first explorers could never be told at all.

In this appendix, extracts from the writings of some of the explorers themselves and of the men who reported their journeys give us a unique view of the courageous pioneers who extended the horizons of the ancient world. Also included are some of the early Greek legends, whose colorful narratives are interwoven with a great deal of geographical knowledge that must have come from voyages made by daring sailors in the remote past.

These documents are followed by a time chart that makes it possible to see at a glance the chronological course of events in different countries and shows what was happening simultaneously in various parts of the known world during the period covered by this book. In this way, the principal explorations may be seen against the background of important historical events.

The next section of the appendix is devoted to concise individual biographies of the explorers, of the geographers who based their knowledge on information collected by the travelers, and of some of the leading historians who recorded their adventures. These biographies are accompanied by line maps to show the routes followed by some of the explorers. A short glossary is provided for quick reference to the meanings of unfamiliar terms, words, and place names that occur in the book.

# The Capture of the Golden Fleece

According to legend, Jason and his band of Greek heroes set sail from Thessaly in northern Greece aboard the swift ship *Argo*. After many adventures, they reached Colchis on the eastern shores of the Black Sea, sailed up the River Phasis (modern Rion), and stole away the Golden Fleece—the gold hide of a sacred ram. This famous narrative is thought to have been woven around a real voyage made by Greek pirates as early as 1250 B.C. The idea of the fleece may have come from the Caucasian practice of using sheepskins to gather gold from the rivers and streams. This account, written in the 200's B.C., describes how Medea, the daughter of the King of Colchis, helped Jason overpower a giant snake and seize the Golden Fleece.

"A path led them to the sacred wood, where they were making for the huge oak on which the fleece was hung. . . . But the serpent with his sharp unsleeping eyes had seen them coming and now confronted them, stretching out his long neck and hissing terribly. . . . But as he writhed he saw the maiden [Medea] take her stand, and heard her in her sweet voice invoking Sleep, the conqueror of the gods, to charm him. . . . Jason from behind looked on in terror. But the giant snake, enchanted by her song, was soon relaxing the whole length of his serrated spine and smoothing out his multitudinous undulations, like a dark and silent swell rolling across a sluggish sea. Yet his

grim head still hovered over them and the cruel jaws threatened to snap them up. But Medea, chanting a spell . . . sprinkled his eyes with her most potent drug; and as the all-pervading magic scent spread round his head, sleep fell on him. Stirring no more, he let his jaw sink to the ground, and his innumerable coils lay stretched out far behind, spanning the deep wood. Medea called to Jason and he snatched the golden fleece from the oak. . . .

"Lord Jason held up the great fleece in his arms. The shimmering wool threw a fiery glow on his fair cheeks and forehead; and he rejoiced in it. . . . The long flocks weighed it down and the very ground before him as he walked was bright with gold. When he slung it on his left shoulder, as he did at times, it reached his feet. But now and again he made a bundle of it in his arms. He was mortally afraid that some god or man might rob him on the way.

"Dawn was spreading over the world when they rejoined the rest. The young men marvelled when they saw the mighty fleece, dazzling as the lightning of Zeus [king of the gods], and they all leapt up in their eagerness to touch it and hold it in their hands. But Jason kept them off and threw a new mantle over the fleece. . . .

" 'My friends,' he said, 'let us start for home without delay. The prize for which we dared greatly and suffered misery on the cruel sea is ours.' "

The Voyage of Argo, Book IV, *Apollonius of Rhodes, trans. by E. V. Rieu (Penguin Books: 1969) pp. 150–152.*

Below: the Argonauts, the group of heroes who sailed with Jason in search of the Golden Fleece. This painting of the adventurers is in Padua, Italy.

Left: the Argonauts, a drawing from an engraved design of the 300's B.C.

Right: a bas-relief of the men who built Jason's ship, the *Argo*.

# Odysseus and the Peril of the Rocks

Below left: Odysseus passing by the temptations of the enticing Sirens. The Sirens were beautiful maidens, whose singing lured sailors to their deaths. Odysseus put wax in his men's ears to prevent them from hearing the Sirens' song.

**Odysseus was the hero of Homer's great epic poem the *Odyssey*. For 10 years, he roamed the unknown seas during his return from the Trojan War to his home on the Greek island of Ithaca. Some of the details of Odysseus' wanderings were probably derived from a number of early voyages in the Mediterranean and Black seas. Here, Odysseus recounts one of the most gruesome ordeals of his journey. He and his crew have to steer their ship through a narrow passage between two rocks (possibly the Strait of Messina between Sicily and Italy). One of the rocks is inhabited by a sea monster with six heads, called Scylla. Beneath the other is a seething whirlpool known as Charybdis.**

"I saw a cloud of smoke ahead and a raging surf, the roar of which I could already hear. My men were so terrified that the oars all dropped from their grasp and fell with a splash in the wash of the ship. . . . I made a tour of the vessel, and with a soothing word for each man I tried to put heart into my company.

" 'My friends,' I said, 'we are men who have met trouble before . . . and I am sure that this too will be a memory for us one day. So now I appeal to you all to do exactly as I say. Oarsmen, stick to your benches, striking hard with your blades through the broken

Right: Odysseus' ship, as it sailed at last into his home port at Ithaca.

Below: the hero Odysseus during his battle with the lion Proteus. Proteus was a Greek sea god, who could change his shape into that of a savage animal, or even into fire or water. If caught and held fast, he would foretell the future.

water, and we may have the luck to slip by and for once avoid disaster. Helmsman. . . . Give a wide berth to that smoke and surf you see, and hug these cliffs. . . .'

"Thus we sailed up the straits, groaning in terror, for on the one side we had Scylla, while on the other the mysterious Charybdis sucked down the salt sea water in her dreadful way. When she vomited it up, she was stirred to her depths and seethed over like a cauldron on a blazing fire; and the spray she flung on high rained down on the tops of the crags at either side. But when she swallowed the salt water down, the whole interior of her vortex was exposed. the rocks re-echoed to her fearful roar, and the dark sands of the sea bottom came into view.

"My men turned pale with fear; and now, while all eyes were fixed on Charybdis and the quarter from which we looked for disaster, Scylla snatched out of my boat the six ablest hands I had on board. I swung round . . . just in time to see the arms and legs of her victims dangled high in the air above my head. 'Odysseus!' they called out to me in agony. But it was the last time they used my name . . . . Scylla had whisked my comrades up and swept them struggling to the rocks, where she devoured them at her own door, shrieking and stretching out their hands to me in their last desperate throes. In all I have gone through as I made my way across the seas, I have never had to witness a more pitiable sight than that."

The Odyssey, Book XII, *Homer, trans. by E. V. Rieu (Penguin Books: 1970) pp. 194–196.*

# Aboard a Phoenician Ship

Above: a terracotta Phoenician mask, which was used in religious ceremonies. Such masks were also placed in tombs to maintain life even in the grave.

**In this account, the Greek soldier-historian Xenophon gives us an interesting glimpse of life aboard a Phoenician ship.**

"Once I had an opportunity of looking over a great Phoenician merchantman . . . and I thought I had never seen tackle so excellently and accurately arranged. . . . As you know, a ship needs a great quantity of wooden and corded implements when she comes into port or puts to sea, much rigging, as it is called, when she sails, many contrivances to protect her against enemy vessels; she carries a large supply of arms for the men, and contains a set of household utensils for each mess. In addition to all this, she is laden with cargo which the skipper carries for profit. And all the things I mention were contained in a chamber of little more than a hundred square cubits [250–300 square feet]. And I noticed that each kind of thing was so neatly stowed away that there was no confusion. . . . I found . . . the steersman's servant . . . in his spare time inspecting all the stores . . . and asked him what he was doing. 'Sir,' he answered, 'I am looking to see how the ship's tackle is stored, in case of accident. . . . For when God sends a storm at sea, there's no time to search about for what you want or to serve it out if it's in a muddle. For God threatens and punishes careless fellows, and you're lucky if he merely refrains from destroying the innocent; and if he saves you when you do your work well, you have cause to thank heaven.'"

Oeconomicus, VIII, 11–16, *Xenophon, trans. by E. C. Marchant. Loeb Classical Library (Harvard University Press and William Heinemann: 1923) pp. 433–435.*

Left: one of the Phoenician warships. This was the type of ship that would have been used for all long journeys.

# The Phoenicians Kidnap a Princess

In the mid-400's B.C, Herodotus wrote the earliest history that has come down to us. His work sets out to trace the events which led to war between Greece and the Persian Empire and to record the history of the known world up to his time. In fact, his books are a unique collection of fascinating information about the histories, legends, customs, and geography of the ancient world. Herodotus questioned everyone he met and wrote about all he heard, whether he believed it or not. His is the only record of the alleged Phoenician voyage around Africa. But that was not all he had to say about the Phoenicians. The first book of his nine-volume *Histories* begins with this account of another unorthodox Phoenician exploit.

"In this book, the result of my enquiries into history, I hope to do two things: to preserve the memory of the past by putting on record the astonishing achievements both of our own and of the Asiatic peoples; secondly, and more particularly, to show how the two races came into conflict.

"Persian historians put the responsibility for the quarrel on the Phoenicians. These people came originally from the coasts of the Indian Ocean; and as soon as they had penetrated into the Mediterranean and settled in that part of the country where they are today, they took to making long trading voyages. Loaded with Egyptian and Assyrian goods, they called at various places along the coast, including Argos, in those days the most important of the countries now called by the general name of Hellas.

"Here in Argos they displayed their wares, and five or six days later when they were nearly sold out, it so happened that a number of women came down to the beach to see the fair. Amongst these was the king's daughter, whom Greek and Persian writers agree in calling Io, daughter of Inachus. These women were standing about near the vessel's stern, buying what they fancied, when suddenly the Phoenician sailors passed the word along and made a rush at them. The greater number got away; but Io and some others were caught and bundled aboard the ship, which cleared at once and made off for Egypt."

The Histories, Book I, *Herodotus, trans. by Aubrey de Sélincourt (Penguin Books: 1968) p. 13.*

Above: a bust of Herodotus, the Father of History, from a woodcut dated 1584.

# The Egyptian Way of Life

Right: some potters and sculptors of ancient Egypt, shaping their works.

**Of all the countries he visited during his travels, Herodotus was most impressed by Egypt, the land that he called the "gift of the Nile." Here, Herodotus gives us an interesting view of everyday life in Egypt in the 400's B.C.**

"Not only is the Egyptian climate peculiar to that country, and the Nile different in its behaviour from other rivers elsewhere, but the Egyptians themselves in their manner and customs seem to have reversed the ordinary practices of mankind. For instance, women attend market and are employed in trade, while men stay at home and do the weaving. . . . No woman holds priestly office, either in the service of goddess or god; only men are priests in both cases. Sons are under no compulsion to support their parents if they do not wish to do so, but daughters must, whether they wish it or not. Elsewhere priests grow their hair long; in Egypt they shave their heads. In other nations the relatives of the deceased in time of mourning cut their hair, but the Egyptians, who shave at all other times, mark a death by letting their hair grow. . . . They live with their animals—unlike the rest of the world, who live apart from them. . . .

"In writing or calculating, instead of going, like the Greeks, from left to right, the Egyptians go from right to left—and obstinately maintain that theirs is the dexterous method, ours being left-handed and awkward. They have two sorts of writing, the sacred and the common. They are religious to excess, beyond any other nation in the world, and here are some of the customs which illustrate the fact; they drink from brazen cups which they scour every day—everyone, without exception. They wear linen clothes which they make a special point of continually washing. . . . The priests, too, wear linen only, and shoes made from the papyrus plant—these materials, for dress and shoes, being the only ones allowed them. They bath in cold water twice a day and twice every night—and observe innumerable other ceremonies besides. . . .

"The Egyptians who live in the cultivated parts of the country, by their practice of keeping records of the past, have made themselves much the best historians of any nation of which I have had experience. I will describe some of their habits: every month for three successive days they purge themselves, for their health's sake . . . in the belief that all diseases come from the food a man eats;

and it is a fact—even apart from this precaution—that next to the Libyans they are the healthiest people in the world. I should put this down myself to the absence of changes in the climate; for change, and especially change of weather, is the prime cause of disease. They eat loaves made from spelt [a type of wheat] . . . and drink a wine made from barley, as they have no vines in the country. Some kinds of fish they eat raw, and ducks and various small birds, after pickling them in brine; other sorts of birds and fish, apart from those which they consider sacred, they either roast or boil. When the rich give a party and the meal is finished, a man carries round amongst the guests a wooden image of a corpse in a coffin, carved and painted to look as much like the real thing as possible, and anything from eighteen inches to three foot long; he shows it to each guest in turn, and says: 'Look upon this body as you drink and enjoy yourself; for you will be just like it when you are dead.' "

The Histories, Book II, *Herodotus, trans. by Aubrey de Sélincourt (Penguin Books: 1968) pp. 115–116, 131.*

Right: two slaves, one African and one Asiatic, painted on the feet of a pharaoh's mummy case, to show that they are perpetually in bondage.

Left: Herodotus reading his *Histories* at a public festival. Like most ancient literature, his work was originally meant to be read aloud to an audience.

# The March of the Ten Thousand

After the Battle of Cunaxa near Babylon when the Greeks routed the Persians in 401 B.C., the Athenian soldier Xenophon was elected commander of the army. Entrusted with leading 10,000 men back safely to their native country, he took them by a northerly route to the Black Sea. Marching over trackless lands, he and his men struggled against death and hunger in their desperate bid to reach the sea. In this extract from his war memoirs, Xenophon recalls some of the dramatic moments of that terrible march. Xenophon wrote his account in the third person and it was first published under a pen name.

"It was a relief to the eyes against snow-blindness if one held something black in front of the eyes while marching; and it was a help to the feet if one kept on the move and never stopped still, and took off one's shoes at night. If one slept with one's shoes on, the straps sank into the flesh and the soles of the shoes froze to the feet. . . . Some soldiers who were suffering from these kinds of complaints were left behind. They had seen a piece of ground that looked black because the snow had gone from it, and they imagined that the snow there had melted—as it actually had done—this being the effect of a fountain which was sending up vapour in a wooded hollow near by. The soldiers turned aside here, sat down, and refused to go any further.

"As soon as Xenophon, who was with the rearguard, heard of this, he begged them, using every argument he could think of, not to get left behind. He told them that there were large numbers of the enemy, formed into bands, who were coming up in the rear, and in the end he got angry. They told him to kill them on the spot, for they could not possibly go on. Under the circumstances the best thing to do seemed to be to scare, if possible, the enemy who were coming up and so prevent them from falling upon the soldiers in their exhausted condition. By this time it was already dark, and the enemy were making a lot of noise as they advanced, quarrelling over the plunder which they had. Then the rearguard, since they had the use of their limbs, jumped up and charged the enemy at the double, while the sick men shouted as hard as they could and clashed their shields against their spears. The enemy were panic-stricken and threw themselves down through the snow into the wooded hollows and not a sound was heard from them afterwards. Xenophon and his troops told the sick men that a detachment would come to help them on the next day, and he then proceeded with the march."

[Several weeks later, Xenophon and his men reach Mount Thekes to the southeast of the Black Sea.]

"When the men in front reached the summit . . . there was great shouting. Xenophon and the rearguard heard it and thought that there were some more enemies attacking in the front. . . . However, when the shouting got louder and drew nearer, and those who were constantly going forward started running towards the men in front who kept on shouting, and the more there were of them the more shouting there was, it looked then as though this was something of considerable importance. So Xenophon mounted his horse and, taking Lycius [commander of cavalry] and the cavalry with him, rode forward to give support, and, quite soon, they heard the soldiers shouting out 'The sea! The sea!' and passing the word down the column. Then certainly they all began to run, the rearguard and all, and drove on the baggage animals and the horses at full speed; and when they had all got to the top, the soldiers, with tears in their eyes, embraced each other and their generals and captains."

The Persian Expedition, Book IV, *Xenophon, trans. by Rex Warner* (*Penguin Books: 1967*) *pp. 151–152, 164–165.*

Left: a bust of the soldier-historian Xenophon, who succeeded in leading his men back to Greece after they had been marooned deep in Persia.

Below: the exciting moment when the soldiers caught their first glimpse of the Black Sea, and realized that they were finally in a place they recognized.

# Alexander Addresses His Troops

Above: the Battle of Malava on the Indus River in 326 B.C. As Alexander was fighting on the wall, the ladder broke and fell from under him.

In 326 B.C., eight years after leaving Macedonia, and having covered about 17,000 miles, Alexander's army reached the extreme eastern limit of the known world. On the frontier of India, Alexander heard of fertile lands beyond the River Hyphasis (modern Beas) and determined to march on. The Greek historian Arrian wrote this account of how Alexander tried to persuade his rebellious men to follow him.

"Reports had come in that the country beyond the Hyphasis was rich and productive. . . . Such stories could not but whet Alexander's appetite for yet another adventure; but his men felt differently. The sight of their king undertaking an endless succession of dangerous and exhausting enterprises was beginning to depress them. Their enthusiasm was ebbing. . . . This state of affairs was brought to Alexander's notice, and before the alarm and despondency among his men could go still further, he called a meeting of his officers and addressed them in the following words:

" 'I observe, gentlemen, that when I would lead you on a new venture you no longer follow me with your old spirit. I have asked you to meet me that we may come to a decision together: are we, upon my advice, to go forward, or, upon yours, to turn back?

" 'If you have any complaint to make about the results of your

Right: Alexander the Great drawing out the plan for his city of Alexandria.

efforts hitherto, or about myself as your commander, there is no more to say. But let me remind you: through your courage and endurance you have gained possession of Ionia, the Hellespont, both Phrygias, Cappadocia, Paphlagonia, Lydia, Caria, Lycia, Pamphylia, Phoenicia, and Egypt; the Greek part of Libya is now yours, together with much of Arabia, lowland Syria, Mesopotamia, Babylon and Susia; Persia and Media with all the territories either formerly controlled by them or not are in your hands; you have made yourselves masters of the lands beyond the Caspian Gates, beyond the Caucasus, beyond the Tanais, of Bactria, Hyrcania, and the Hyrcanian Sea; we have driven the Scythians back into the desert; and Indus and Hydaspes, Acesines, and Hydraotes flow now through country which is ours. With all that accomplished, why do you hesitate to extend the power of Macedon—*your* power—to the Hyphasis and the tribes on the other side? . . .

" 'I could not have blamed you for being the first to lose heart if I, your commander, had not shared your exhausting marches and your perilous campaigns. . . . But it is not so. You and I, gentlemen, have shared the labour and shared the danger, and the rewards are for us all. The conquered territory belongs to you; from your ranks the governors of it are chosen; already the greater part of its treasure passes into your hands, and when all Asia is overrun . . . the utmost hopes of riches or power which each one of you cherishes will be far surpassed, and whoever wishes to return home will be allowed to go, either with me or without me. I will make those who stay the envy of those who return.'

"When Alexander ended, there was a long silence. The officers present were not willing to accept what he had said, yet no one liked to risk an unprepared reply."

The Life of Alexander the Great, Book V, 25–27, *Arrian, trans. by Aubrey de Sélincourt (Penguin Books: 1962) pp. 187–189.*

Above: Alexander's horse, Bucephalus, which he had trained himself. He took Bucephalus to India with his army.

Below: Mankiala Stupa near Rāwalpindi in Pakistan. According to legend, Mankiala Stupa is the tomb of Alexander's horse, Bucephalus.

# Hannibal in the Alps

**Even when Hannibal was over the highest point in his crossing of the Alps in 218 B.C., the downward progress of his army into Italy was beset with hazards. The descent being shorter was correspondingly steeper, and the going much more difficult. This record of those perilous moments was written by a Roman, the historian Livy. Hannibal left no personal reports, and the accounts of his expedition which have survived all come from his Roman enemies. No matter how biased Roman accounts of the campaign may be, however, they all acknowledge Hannibal's outstanding military genius.**

"The track was almost everywhere precipitous, narrow, and slippery; it was impossible for a man to keep his feet; the least stumble meant a fall, and a fall a slide, so that there was indescribable confusion, men and beasts stumbling and slipping on top of each other.

"Soon they found themselves on the edge of a precipice—a narrow cliff falling away so sheer that even a lightly-armed soldier could hardly have got down it by feeling his way and clinging to such bushes and stumps as presented themselves. It must always have been a most awkward spot, but a recent landslide had converted it on this occasion to a perpendicular drop of nearly a thousand feet. On the brink the cavalry drew rein—their journey seemed to be over. Hannibal, in the rear, did not yet know what had brought the column to a halt; but when the message was passed to him that there was no possibility of proceeding, he went in person to reconnoitre. It was clear to him that a detour would have to be made, however long it might prove to be, over the trackless and untrodden slopes in the vicinity. But even so he was no luckier; progress was impossible, for though there was good foothold in the quite shallow layer of soft fresh snow which had covered the old snow underneath, nevertheless as soon as it had been trampled and dispersed by the feet of all those men and animals, there was left to tread upon only the bare ice and liquid slush of melting snow underneath. The result was a horrible struggle, the ice affording no foothold in any case, and least of all on a steep slope; when a man tried by hands or knees to get on his feet again, even those useless supports slipped from under him and let him down; there were no stumps or roots anywhere to afford a purchase to either foot or hand; in short, there was nothing for it but to roll and slither on the smooth ice and melting

Above: Hannibal's soldiers ferrying his elephants across a river on rafts.

Above right: Livy, the historian who recorded the exploits of Hannibal.

Left: Hannibal, the general of Carthage who defied Rome and all its power in his effort to keep his city independent.

snow. Sometimes the mules' weight would drive their hoofs through into the lower layer of old snow. . . .

"When it became apparent that both men and beasts were wearing themselves out to no purpose, a space was cleared—with the greatest labour because of the amount of snow to be dug and carted away—and camp was pitched, high up on the ridge. The next task was to construct some sort of passable track down the precipice, for by no other route could the army proceed. It was necessary to cut through rock, a problem they solved by the ingenious application of heat and moisture; large trees were felled and lopped, and a huge pile of timber erected; this, with the opportune help of a strong wind, was set on fire, and when the rock was sufficiently heated the men's rations of sour wine were flung upon it, to render it friable. They then got to work with picks on the heated rock and opened a sort of zigzag track, to minimize the steepness of the descent, and were able, in consequence, to get the pack animals, and even the elephants, down it."

The War with Hannibal, Book XXI, 35–37, *Livy, trans. by Aubrey de Sélincourt (Penguin Books: 1970) pp. 61–62.*

# Caesar Invades Britain

In 55 B.C., Julius Caesar invaded Britain. At the head of an army of 10,000 men, he sailed across the English Channel from Gaul and landed at Walmer in Kent, southeast England. This is Caesar's own account of his first encounter with the Britons. Like Xenophon, Caesar writes his memoirs in the third person.

"Caesar himself reached Britain with the first ships about nine o'clock in the morning, and saw the enemy's forces posted on all the hills. The lie of the land at this point was such that javelins could be hurled from the cliffs right on to the narrow beach enclosed between them and the sea. Caesar thought this a quite unsuitable place for landing, and therefore rode at anchor until three o'clock,

in order to give the rest of the ships time to come up. Meanwhile he assembled the generals and military tribunes, and explained his plans. . . . On dismissing the officers he found that both wind and tidal current were in his favour. He therefore gave the signal for weighing anchor, and after proceeding about seven miles ran his ships aground on an evenly sloping beach, free from obstacles.

"The natives, on realizing his intention, had sent forward their cavalry and a number of the chariots which they are accustomed to use in warfare; the rest of their troops followed close behind and

Below: these somewhat fanciful drawings of ancient Britons, many of them with tattooed bodies, are taken from an edition of Caesar's *Commentaries* published in the 1600's.

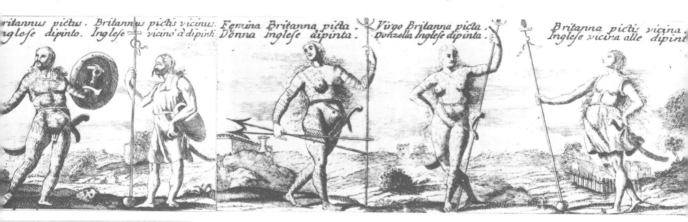

were ready to oppose the landing. The Romans were faced with very grave difficulties. The size of the ships made it impossible to run them aground except in fairly deep water; and the soldiers, unfamiliar with the ground, with their hands full, and weighed down by the heavy burden of their arms, had at the same time to jump down from the ships, get a footing in the waves, and fight the enemy, who, standing on dry land or advancing only a short way into the water, fought with all their limbs unencumbered and on perfectly familiar ground, boldly hurling javelins and galloping their horses, which were trained to this kind of work. These perils frightened our soldiers, who were quite unaccustomed to battles of this kind. . . .

"Seeing this, Caesar ordered the warships—which were swifter and easier to handle than the transports . . . to be rowed hard and run ashore on the enemy's right flank. . . . Scared by the strange shape of the warships . . . the natives halted and then retreated a little. But as the Romans still hesitated, chiefly on account of the depth of the water, the man who carried the eagle of the 10th legion . . . cried out in a loud voice: 'Jump down, comrades, unless you want to surrender our eagle to the enemy. . . .' With these words he leapt out of the ship and advanced towards the enemy with the eagle in his hands. At this the soldiers, exhorting each other not to submit to such a disgrace, jumped with one accord from the ship, and the men from the next ships, when they saw them, followed them and advanced against the enemy."

The Conquest of Gaul *Caesar, trans. by S. A. Handford (Penguin Books: 1970) pp. 121–122.*

# Hsuan-tsang Crosses the Gobi

**Defying the emperor's orders, the Chinese Buddhist Hsuan-tsang set out in the A.D. 600's to travel from China to India. The first part of his long journey lay across the bleak wastes of the Gobi Desert. Even today, with the aid of modern equipment, such a journey would be a daunting prospect. For Hsuan-tsang it was doubly dangerous, because he ran the constant risk of being arrested by frontier guards. This extract from a biography of Hsuan-tsang (the Master of the Law), written by one of his disciples, describes his experiences in the desert.**

"And now, alone and deserted, he traversed the sandy waste; his only means of observing the way being the heaps of bones and the horse-dung, and so on; thus slowly and cautiously advancing, he suddenly saw a body of troops, amounting to several hundreds, covering the sandy plain; sometimes they advanced and sometimes they halted. The soldiers were clad in fur and felt. And now the appearance of camels and horses, and the glittering of standards and lances met his view; then suddenly fresh forms and figures changing into a thousand shapes appeared, sometimes at an immense distance and then close at hand, and then they dissolved into nothing.

"The Master of the Law when he first beheld the sight thought they were robbers, but when he saw them come near and vanish, he knew that they were the hallucinations of demons. Again, he heard in the void sounds of voices crying out: 'Do not fear! do not fear!' On this he composed himself, and having pushed on eighty *li* or so [about 27 miles], he saw the first watch-tower [Chinese frontier post]. Fearing lest the lookouts should see him, he concealed himself in a hollow of sand until night; then going on west of the tower, he saw the water; and going down, he drank and washed his hands. Then as he was filling his water-vessel with water an arrow whistled past him and just grazed his knee, and in a moment another arrow. Knowing then that he was discovered, he cried with a loud voice: 'I am a priest come from the capital; do not shoot me!' Then he led his horse towards the tower, whilst the men on guard opening the gate, came out; after looking at him they saw that he was indeed a priest, and so they entered in together to see the commander of the guard-house. . . . [Hsuan-tsang is allowed to spend the night at the frontier post and the following night at the next post.]

Left: a stone carving showing gods
worshiping a turban, a relic of
the Buddha. The lower panel shows
the Buddha enthroned in splendor.

"Having gone from this he forthwith entered on the *Mo-kia-Yen* desert [Taklamakan], which is about 800 *li* [267 miles] in extent. The old name for it is Sha-ho. There are no birds overhead, and no beasts below; there is neither water nor herb to be found. . . .

"After going a hundred *li* or so, he lost his way. . . . Then when he was going to drink from the pipe of his water-vessel, because of its weight it slipped from his hands, and the water was wasted; thus, a supply enough for 1,000 *li* was lost in a moment. Then again, because of the winding character of the road, he did not know which way to follow it. . . .

"At this time . . . in the four directions, the view was boundless; there were no traces either of man or horse, and in the night the demons and goblins raised fire-lights as many as the stars; in the day-time the driving wind blew the sand before it as in the season of rain. But notwithstanding all this his heart was unaffected by fear; but he suffered from want of water, and was so parched with thirst that he could no longer go forward. Thus for four nights and five days not a drop of water had he to wet his throat or mouth; his stomach was racked with a burning heat, and he was well-nigh thoroughly exhausted. And now not being able to advance he lay down to rest on the sands. . . .

"With earnest heart and without cessation [he prayed] the while, till the middle of the fifth night, when suddenly a cool wind fanned his body, cold and refreshing as a bath of icy water. . . .

"The Master of the Law, rousing himself from slumber, pushed on for ten *li*, when his horse suddenly started off another way and could not be brought back or turned. Having gone some *li* in the new direction, he saw all at once several acres of green grass; getting off his horse, he let him graze; when leaving the grass, purposing to resume his journey, about ten paces off he came to a pool of water, sweet, and bright as a mirror; dismounting again, he drank without stint, and so his body and vital powers were restored once more. . . .

"Having bivouacked near the grass and fountain of water for a day, on the day following he filled his water-vessel and cut some grass, and proceeded onward. After two days more they got out of the desert. . . ."

The Life of Hiuen-tsiang, Book I, *Hwui Li, ed. by Samuel Beal (Kegan Paul, Trench, Trubner & Co. Ltd.: London, 1911) pp. 18–24.*

# Time Chart

| | 4000 – 2000 | 2000 – 1500 | 1500 – 1000 | 1000 – 600 | 600 – 40... |
|---|---|---|---|---|---|
| **MINOANS** | 3400 Beginning of Minoan civilization<br>Foundation of Mediterranean sea travel | Contact with Egypt established<br>Trade and manufacture flourish | 1500-1400 Golden Age of Crete<br>Regular trade with Egypt<br>1400 Fall of Crete | | |
| **PHOENICIANS** | 2756 Tyre founded<br><br>2600 Cedars of Lebanon exported to Egypt | Ugarit becomes first great international port | Phoenicians take over from the Minoans sea dominance of the Mediterranean<br>Great colonizing and trading era<br>1000 Invention of the alphabet | 950 Voyage to Ophir for Solomon<br>814 Traditional date for founding of Carthage<br>668 Tyre conquered by Assyrians<br>600 Reported circumnavigation of Africa for Necho of Egypt | 573 Tyre capitulate Nebuchadnez<br>Carthage dom Mediterranean<br>450 Hanno's color expedition dow west coast of A<br>Himilco's four month voyage Atlantic |
| **EGYPTIANS** | 3100 Upper and Lower Egypt united<br>3000 Pyramid building begins<br>2600 Sneferu orders earliest recorded voyage to Byblos<br>2500 Voyage to Punt under Sahure<br>2007 Voyage to Punt led by Hennu | 1890 Nile-Red Sea canal built by Sesostris II | 1493 Queen Hatshepsut's expedition to Punt<br>1450 Thutmose III marches to Euphrates River<br>1080 Wen-Amun travels to Byblos for cedars<br>Egyptian power declines | 712 Trading relations opened with Greece<br>600 Necho tries to re-open canal between Nile and Red Sea Also believed to have sent Phoenicians around Africa | 525 Egypt conque Persians<br>505 Darius the Gre reopens Nile-F Sea canal |
| **GREEKS** | | 2000 First Greek-speaking people probably enter Greek mainland<br>1500 Rise of Mycenaean civilization<br>Beginning of Heroic Age portrayed in Homer's poems | 1200 Siege of Troy<br>1120 Dorian invasion<br>End of Mycenaean civilization | 750 Colonization of Asia Minor<br>Exploration of the Black Sea<br>Settlements in Egypt and Sicily<br>630 Colaeus enters the Atlantic<br>600 Massalia founded<br>Silver trade with Tartessus | 546 Anaximander first map of the<br>510 Scylax sails do Indus River an around Arabia the Red Sea<br>463-431 Golden A Athens<br>460 Herodotus tra collect inform for his *Historie*<br>431-404 Pelopon War betw Athens a Sparta |
| **ROMANS** | | First farmers settle in Po Valley | 1000 Etruscan civilization begins in western Italy | 753 Traditional founding of Rome by Romulus and Remus | Etruscans rule<br>509 Romans rise a Etruscans<br>Roman Repul declared<br>Internal politi organization |
| **CHINESE** | 2700 Legendary discovery of silk | 2000 Emergence of Chinese civilization<br>1500 Beginning of Shang dynasty | Growth of cities | Shang dynasty falls to Chou warriors | Chinese Empire ex under Chou dynas |

| 400 – 300 | 300 – 200 | 200 – 1 B.C. | A.D. 1 – 300 | 300 – 700 |
|---|---|---|---|---|
| Tyre captured by Alexander<br><br>Final collapse of Phoenicia | 264-241 First Punic War<br><br>237 Carthaginians settle in Spain<br><br>218 Second Punic War begins<br><br>218 Hannibal crosses Alps<br><br>202 Carthaginians defeated<br><br>Spain surrendered to Rome | 149 Third Punic War<br><br>Carthage besieged<br><br>146 Carthage destroyed | | |
| Egypt annexed by Alexander<br><br>Founding of Alexandria<br><br>Ptolemy Soter I founds Ptolemaic dynasty | Alexandria becomes leading cultural and commercial center | 48 Caesar enters Alexandria<br><br>30 Egypt becomes a province of the Roman Empire | Regular trading voyages from Egypt to India ordered by Romans | 641 Egypt conquered by Moslems |
| Xenophon's journey with the Ten Thousand<br><br>Alexander begins his 11 years of conquest and exploration<br><br>Nearchus explores Persian Gulf<br><br>Pytheas circumnavigates Britain | 296 Wars of Alexander's successors for supremacy over his dominions<br><br>211 War between Greek cities | 146 Greece becomes Roman province<br><br>120 Eudoxus sent by Euergetes II to find sea route from Egypt to India | 60-70 Diogenes said to have found source of Nile<br><br>120 Alexander reaches China by sea<br><br>150? Ptolemy publishes his Geography<br><br>255 Goths invade Greece | 529 Justinian closes schools of philosophy in Athens<br><br>Alexandria remains center of Greek knowledge |
| Capture of Etruscan city of Veii after 10-year siege<br><br>Gauls sack Rome and occupy city for seven months<br><br>War begins against Samnites (tribe from Apennines)<br><br>Rome victorious over the Latin League (group of cities formerly allied to Rome) | 290 Samnites crushed<br><br>275 Greek cities in southern Italy conquered<br><br>Rome supreme in Italy<br><br>239 Rome in command of western Mediterranean<br><br>Relations with Greece established<br><br>214 Beginning of Roman conquest in the Aegean | 146 Carthage destroyed, Greece annexed<br><br>66 Pompey explores lands between Caspian and Black seas<br><br>58-50 Caesar conquers Gaul<br><br>55-54 Caesar's expeditions to Britain<br><br>47 Caesar conquers Egypt<br><br>27 Founding of Roman Empire<br><br>25 Gallus explores southern Arabia | 42 Suetonius Paulinus crosses Atlas mountains<br><br>43 Claudius' expedition to Britain<br><br>61 Nero's expedition up the Nile<br><br>70 Romans destroy Jerusalem<br><br>70-80 Agricola's expedition to Britain | 330 Founding of Constantinople<br><br>337 Christianity becomes official religion of Roman Empire<br><br>476 End of Roman Empire in West<br><br>540 Justinian fixes price of silk and orders smuggling of silk-worms' eggs from China<br><br>Silk production begins in the West |
| se Empire expands Chou dynasty | 221 Chou dynasty replaced by Ch'in dynasty<br><br>221-207 Great Wall of China built<br><br>206 Beginning of rule by Han dynasty | 141-87 Wu Ti extends China's boundaries<br><br>138 Chang Ch'ien leaves China on his 20-year travels<br><br>105 Opening up of Silk Road | 166 First embassy to China from Rome<br><br>221 Han dynasty falls | Wars with invading Turko-Mongol tribes<br><br>400 Fa-Hsien travels to central India<br><br>453 Buddhism adopted as state religion<br><br>629 Hsuan-Tsang begins his travels |

# The Explorers

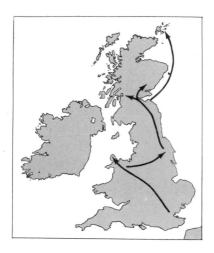

## AGRICOLA, GNAEUS JULIUS
A.D. 37–93                           Rome
70–80: Commanded Roman forces in Britain. Conquered northern England and North Wales. Explored coast of Scotland and probably sent a fleet to sail around Britain. Was appointed governor of Britain. Planned to invade Ireland but was recalled to Rome.

## ALEXANDER THE GREAT
356–323 B.C.                    Macedonia
334–329 B.C.: Led about 35,000 men from Macedonia across the Hellespont (Dardanelles) to invade the Persian Empire. Visited the site of Troy. Defeated the Persians on the banks of the Granicus River. Won back for the Greeks the Persian-occupied cities on the eastern shores of the Aegean Sea. Marched inland, crossed the Taurus Mountains, and returned to the coast at Taurus on the Mediterranean. Defeated Darius III of Persia at Issus, near the Turkish-Syrian frontier. Occupied Phoenicia. Captured Tyre. Marched into Egypt, where he founded the city of Alexandria. Returned to Tyre and pushed on through Syria. Defeated the Persians at Gaugamela near the ruins of Nineveh (in modern Iraq). Continued south through Babylon to Susa (in what is now southwest Iran). Seized the Persian capital of Persepolis.

Pursued Darius northward to Ecbatana (present-day Hamadan in Iran) and on to Damghan, just south of the Elburz Mountains. Advanced to Kabul in eastern Afghanistan and marched over the Hindu Kush. Crossed the Oxus (Amu-Darya) River to Sogdiana.
329–327 B.C.: Marched northward as far as Samarkand and the Jaxartes (Syr-Darya) River in Soviet Central Asia. Explored large regions of what are now Afghanistan and the Uzbek and Turkmen republics of the U.S.S.R.
327–326 B.C.: Led his men across the mountains between Afghanistan and West Pakistan. Reached the Indus and marched on to the Hydaspes (Jhelum) River, where he defeated King Porus. Continued eastward across the Punjab to the Hyphasis (Beas) River, about 250 miles northwest of modern Delhi. There, his army refused to march on, and he led them back to the Hydaspes.
326–323 B.C.: Sailed down the Hydaspes and Acesines (Chenāb) rivers to the Indus and reached the Arabian Sea. Sent part of the army by sea with Nearchus, the sick and the wounded overland with Craterus, and marched with the remainder of his troops along the coast of present-day West Pakistan, through the Makrān Desert and on to Bandar-e Shāhpūr (in southeastern Iran). Marched inland to Persepolis and on to Susa. Sent expeditions to explore the Caspian Sea and sailed down the Euphrates River. Went to Babylon, where he died of fever.
*See map on page 93*

## ARRIAN (FLAVIUS ARRIANUS)
A.D. 96(?)–180(?)                Greece
131–137: Although a Greek, he was appointed governor of the Roman province of Cappadocia (now in central Turkey) by the Emperor Hadrian.
147–148: *Archon* (chief magistrate) at Athens. Retired to his home town of Nicomedia (modern Izmit in northwestern Turkey) and devoted the remainder of his life to writing. His chief work was the *Anabasis of Alexander,* a history of Alexander the Great.

## CAESAR, GAIUS JULIUS
100(?)–44 B.C.                      Rome
59 B.C.: Elected consul and ruled Rome in alliance with Crassus and Pompey.
58 B.C.: Began his nine-year campaign in Gaul during which he conquered what is now France, southern Holland, Belgium, most of Switzerland, and the part of Germany west of the Rhine River.
55 B.C.: Led about 10,000 men across the English Channel to invade Britain. Landed in Kent, southeast England; and marched a short distance inland. Retreated to Gaul after two weeks.
54 B.C.: Invaded Britain a second time. Landed with about 30,000 men near Sandwich in Kent. Marched westward through Kent and defeated the Britons near present-day Canterbury. Crossed the River Medway. Followed the River Thames, which he crossed probably somewhere below present-day London. Marched on to St. Albans (about 20 miles northwest of London). Returned after three months to resume war in Gaul.
49 B.C.: Led his troops across the Rubicon River between Gaul and Italy, and marched on Rome. Became master of Italy.
48–45 B.C.: Defeated Pompey at Pharsalus in Greece. Pursued Pompey to Egypt, where he met Cleopatra. Crushed Pompey's supporters in Africa, Asia, and Europe.
44 B.C.: Murdered in Rome on March 15 (the Ides of March).
*See map on page 118*

## CHANG CH'IEN
100's B.C.                          China
138–126 B.C.: Sent by the Emperor Wu Ti on a journey into central Asia to contact the Yue-Chi. Imprisoned for 10 years by the Huns. Escaped and traveled westward to Bactria (now northern Afghanistan), where he found the Yue-Chi. Tried to return to China by way of Tibet but was again captured by the Huns. Escaped and reached China.
105 B.C.: Made a reconnaissance expedition that resulted in the opening up of the Silk Road.
*See map on page 136*

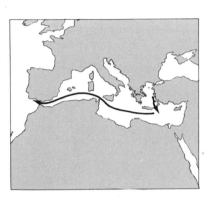

## COLAEUS
600's B.C.            Greece
630 B.C.: Set out from his native
island of Samos in the Aegean Sea to
sail to Egypt. Was blown off course
by an east wind and driven across the
Mediterranean and through the Strait
of Gibraltar. In this way, he became
the first Greek to reach the Atlantic
Ocean. Landed at Tartessus in
southern Spain and sold his cargo. After
his return to Asia Minor, reports of
his discovery opened the way for
trade between the Aegean and Spain.

## COSMAS
A.D. 500's            Greece
Early 500's: An Egyptian Greek, born
in Alexandria, he became a merchant
traveler. Traded in Ethiopia and
Persia and went as far as western
India and Ceylon.
535( ?)–547( ?): Became a monk and
returned to Alexandria, where he wrote
*Christian Topography.* In this book
he attacked the belief that the earth
is a sphere. He represented the
universe as a rectangular box, within
which the inhabited world rose from
an ocean surrounded by Eden.

## DIOGENES
dates unknown            Greece
60( ?)–70( ?): Said to have been the
first to discover the true sources of
the Nile. Returning from a trading
voyage to India, he was driven off
course and landed on the east coast
of Africa near modern Dar es Salaam,
Tanzania. Traveled inland for 25

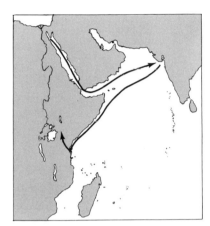

days and reached two great lakes
(possibly Victoria and Albert), which
he claimed to be the sources of the
Nile. In his report of Diogenes' journey,
the Greek geographer Ptolemy
recorded that these lakes were fed by
melted snow from nearby mountains
called the Mountains of the Moon.

## EUDOXUS
dates unknown            Greece
120 B.C.( ?): Traveled from his home
in Cyzicus (modern Kapidagi in
northwestern Turkey) to Alexandria.
Sent by the Greek ruler of Egypt,
Euergetes II, to explore sea route from
Egypt to India (previously sailed in
reverse direction by Scylax but since
forgotten). Guided by an Indian pilot, he
reached India and returned with a
rich cargo.
117 B.C.( ?): Sailed again from Egypt
to India. On return voyage was blown

off course and landed on Somali coast
of East Africa. Finally reached
Alexandria.
108( ?)–105 B.C.( ?): Set out to try
to sail around Africa from west to
east. Abandoned the expedition off
the coast of Morocco and made his
way back to Gades (Cádiz). Left
Gades on another attempt but nothing
more was ever heard of him.

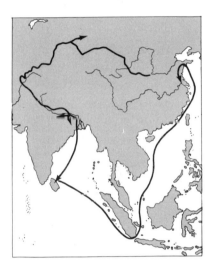

## FA-HSIEN
dates unknown            China
A.D. 400–415: Led a party of Chinese
Buddhists on a pilgrimage to India.
Traveled for six years from Changan
to Khotan (western China), across the
Pamirs, and on into Kashmir. Spent
a further six years in India, sailing
down the Ganges River, visiting
monasteries, and copying sacred books.
Traveled to Ceylon. Returned to
China by sea.

## GALLUS, AELIUS
dates unknown            Rome
25–24 B.C.: Sent by the Emperor
Augustus to invade southern Arabia.
Sailed with 10,000 men from
Cleopatris, near present-day Suez, and
landed about 300 miles down the
Arabian coast. Marched southward
across the Arabian desert. Tried to find
the city of Marib, near modern Ṣanʻāʼ

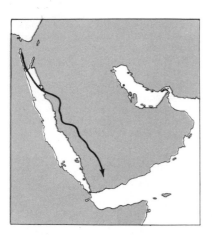

in central Yemen, which was said to
have been the Queen of Sheba's
capital. Besieged a city called Mariba
(possibly not the same place as the
legendary Marib) but failed to capture
it. Retreated across the desert. The
expedition was a failure, and, although
Gallus returned safely, many of his men
died from disease and exhaustion.
*See map on page 118*

## HANNIBAL
247–183 B.C.                    Carthage
237 B.C.: Left Carthage for southern
Spain.
218 B.C.: Marched from Cartagena,
southeast Spain, with an army of
72,000 men and 37 elephants.
Crossed the Pyrenees into southern
Gaul (France). Struck northward up the
Rhône Valley and crossed the Rhône
probably at Fourques, near Arles.
Believed to have followed the Rhône
to its junction with the Drôme River
and then turned eastward to the Alps.
Crossed the Alps in 15 days, probably
by the 9,000-foot-high southern pass,
the Col de la Traversette, east of
Gap. Descended into the plains of
Northern Italy.
203 B.C.: Withdrew his unconquered
army from Italy and returned to
Carthage.
202 B.C.: Defeated by Scipio Africanus
at Zama, southwest of modern Tunis
in North Africa.
183 B.C.: Committed suicide to

escape capture by the Romans.
*See map on page 118*

## HANNO
dates unknown                    Carthage
450 B.C. ( ? ): Led a colonizing voyage
down the west coast of Africa. Set
out from Carthage with 30,000
settlers in 60 ships. Sailed through the
Strait of Gibraltar and founded a
colony at Thymiaterium (modern
Mehedia, north of Casablanca in
Morocco). Continued southward along
Moroccan coast, founding six more
towns. Landed at the mouth of a
river (probably the Draâ near the
southern border of Morocco). Sailed
along coast of Spanish Sahara and
left remaining settlers on an island
called Cerne (possibly Herne Island
off Spanish Sahara, Arguin Island off
Mauritania, or an island near the mouth
of the Senegal River). Explored the
Chretes River (probably the Senegal)
and then resumed the voyage south.
Probably landed on one of the
Bissagos Islands off Portuguese Guinea.
Continued down the coast and sighted
the "Chariot of the Gods" (thought to
be Mount Kakulima or Mount
Cameroon).
Landed on another island (possibly
Sherbro Island off Sierra Leone).
Probably sailed as far as present-day
border between Sierra Leone and
Liberia but may have gone as far
south as Gabon.

## HATSHEPSUT
reigned 1503( ?)–1482 B.C.        Egypt
1493 B.C.: Sent an expedition to Punt
under the command of Nehsi. Her ships
may have been carried across the
desert from Coptos (modern Kuft), on
the east bank of the Nile, to the Red
Sea, or have sailed down the Nile and
through a canal to the head of the
Gulf of Suez. They traveled southward
down the Red Sea and the east coast
of Africa to Punt (probably Somaliland
but possibly as far south as
Mozambique).
Returned to Egypt with a rich cargo.
1485 B.C.: Ordered an expedition up
the Nile to the granite quarries at
the First Cataract (Aswan) for two huge
obelisks. Each obelisk was $97\frac{1}{2}$ feet
long and weighed 350 tons. The
obelisks were loaded onto a barge and
towed about 150 miles down the Nile
to Thebes by 30 boats. One of the
obelisks still stands at the great temple
at Karnak on the east bank of the Nile.
*See map on page 27*

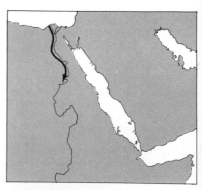

## HERODOTUS
484( ?)–424 B.C.( ?)              Greece
464( ?)–447 B.C.( ?): Left his home in
Halicarnassus (modern Bodrum in
southwestern Turkey) to travel in search
of firsthand information for his
*Histories.* Visited Greece and the
Aegean islands. Traveled from Sardis to
Susa and Babylon. Went to Colchis on
the southeastern shores of the Black
Sea. Explored the western shores of the
Black Sea as far as the Dnepr River
in southern Russia. Visited Scythia,
which lay to the north and northeast

of the Black Sea. Traveled to southern
Italy. Visited Phoenicia and made a
long stay in Egypt. Lived for several
years on the Aegean island of Samos
and then returned to Halicarnassus.
447(?)–444 B.C.(?): Lived in Athens
where his books were read aloud to
large audiences.
444 B.C.(?): Sailed from Athens with
a group of Greek settlers who founded
a colony at Thurii in southern Italy.
Remained in Thurii until his death
in about 424 B.C.

## HIMILCO
dates unknown                    Carthage
450 B.C.(?): Set out from Gades
(modern Cádiz in southwest Spain) on
a voyage to the North Atlantic in search
of the Tin Islands. Probably sailed
up the Atlantic coast of Spain, followed
the French coast to Brittany and
crossed the English Channel to the
Scilly Islands off southwest England.
May have reached the British mainland.
Returned to Gades after four months.

## HIPPALUS
dates unknown                        Greece
About 45 B.C.: Sailed from Egypt to
India across the open sea. Although
he was not the first to use the

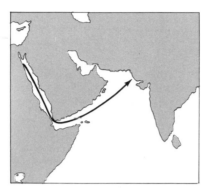

monsoon route, he has sometimes
been credited with its discovery.
His name was given to the southwest
monsoon, to an African cape, and to
the southern part of the Gulf of Oman.

## HSUAN-TSANG
A.D. 610(?)–(?)                    China
629(?)–645(?): A Buddhist monk, he
left China to visit Buddhist sanctuaries
in India. Crossed the Gobi Desert,
and made his way over the Tien Shan
mountains to Tashkent. Traveled
on to Samarkand. Crossed the Oxus
River and visited Buddhist monasteries
in Bactria. Went over the Hindu Kush
and through the Khyber Pass to
Peshāwar (in what is now northern
West Pakistan). Explored the Swat
Valley and crossed the Indus Rover.
Spent two years in Kashmir, then
continued to the Ganges River. Spent
several years visiting cities, monasteries,
and libraries. Journeyed southward
across the Deccan and northward along
the west coast of the Bay of Bengal.
Traveled through Assam in northeast
India and then set out across the
Punjab on return to China. Made his
way up the valley of the Oxus.
Crossed the Pamirs to Kashgar in
western China. Followed the Silk Road
to Khotan and across the Taklamakan
desert. Reached the Chinese capital,
where he was received in triumph.
Spent the rest of his life translating
religious manuscripts from India.
See map on page 136

## NEARCHUS
(?)–about 312 B.C.                    Crete

327–326 B.C.: Supervised the building
of a fleet for Alexander on the banks
of the Hydaspes (Jhelum) River.
325–324 B.C.: Sailed down the Indus
with Alexander. Took command of 150
ships carrying about 5,000 of Alexander's men. Sailed from the mouth
of the Indus to the mouth of the
Euphrates at the head of the Persian
Gulf in 130 days. Sailed back as far
as Bandar-e Shāhpūr in modern Iran,
and marched inland to rejoin Alexander
on the route to Persepolis.
See map on page 93

## NECHO II
reigned 609–594 B.C.                    Egypt
About 600 B.C.: Tried to open a canal
from a point near Bubastis on the
Nile Delta to the Red Sea. Abandoned
the attempt (said to have cost the
lives of 120,000 men) when warned by
an oracle that the canal would help
the Persians to invade Egypt. According
to Herodotus, he sent Phoenician
sailors to sail around Africa to find a
sea route from the Red Sea to the
Mediterranean. The Phoenicians
are reported to have set out from a port
on the Red Sea, rounded Africa, and
returned to Egypt in about three years.

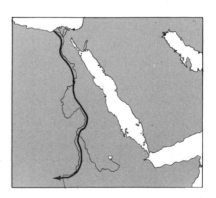

## NERO
A.D. 37–68                        Rome
61: Sent an expedition to explore the
upper reaches of the Nile and try to
find its source. The expedition, led
by two centurions, probably followed
a caravan route up the Nile to the

Dunqulah bend in present-day Sudan, and then cut across the desert to rejoin the river just below modern Khartoum. They finally reached the *sudd,* a mass of vegetation blocking the river, and were forced to turn back.

## PLINY THE ELDER
A.D. 23–79                    Rome
Born in Novum Comum (present-day Como) in northern Italy but moved to Rome as a young man. Became a writer and lawyer. Wrote over 100 historical, scientific, and military works. Of these, only his 37-volume *Natural History* has survived. It is an encyclopedia of scientific knowledge and includes volumes on geography.

## POLYBIUS
204( ?)–122 B.C.( ?)          Greece
168 B.C.: Taken to Rome as a political prisoner after the Roman conquest of Macedonia.
147–146 B.C.: Went to North Africa, where he witnessed the destruction of Carthage by the Romans.
146–124 B.C.( ?):Devoted himself to writing his 40-volume *Histories,* dealing with the history of the Roman Republic from 266 to 146 B.C. Traveled in Egypt, Numidia (part of present-day Algeria), Spain, and Gaul to collect firsthand information. Followed Hannibal's entire route before writing an account of his expedition. Only the first five of Polybius' books, and fragments of some of the others, have survived.

## PTOLEMY
dates unknown                 Greece
About A.D. 150: An astronomer, mathe-matician, and geographer, Ptolemy is thought to have spent most of his life at Alexandria in Egypt. Wrote a 13-volume work called *Mathematical Composition* (also known as *Almagest*) containing his astronomical theories. Believed that the earth was round and motionless, and that the sun, moon, and planets traveled around it at varying speeds. Visualized the stars as spots of light in a concave roof that arched over the universe like a dome. In his *Geography,* consisting of eight books, he set out his theory of map projection and listed 8,000 towns, rivers, and mountains giving their latitudes and, in some cases, their longitudes. The work is accompanied by an atlas of maps, but these may have been elaborated later from rough sketches made by Ptolemy. Ptolemy's *Geography* contained the sum of geographical knowledge up to his time and remained virtually unchallenged until the 1400's.
*See map on page 155*

## PTOLEMY I SOTER
367( ?)–283 B.C.              Macedonia
334–323 B.C.: Served as general under Alexander and was one of his favorite companions. Wrote a biography (now lost) of Alexander which was used by Arrian as his main source.
323 B.C.: After Alexander's death, took Egypt and Libya as his share of the empire. Added Syria to his territory in 312 B.C.
305 B.C.: Took the title of king of Egypt. Made Alexandria his capital. Developed the city into a leading center of learning and founded a great library and museum there. Extended his rule to Cyrene, Crete, and Cyprus.

## PYTHEAS
dates unknown                 Greece
About 325 B.C.: Left his home in the Greek colony of Massalia (modern Marseille) on a journey to the North Atlantic. May have traveled across France, but probably sailed through the Strait of Gibraltar and around the Iberian Peninsula to the island of Ushant off the tip of Brittany in northwest France. Probably struck across the English Channel to Land's End in Cornwall, southwest England. Circumnavigated Britain, measuring its coasts, and making several landings. Received reports of an island called Thule (probably Iceland or Norway), said to be the northern limit of the world. May have visited Thule. Thought to have explored the Rhine River and may have entered the Baltic Sea. Nothing is known of his return journey to Massalia.
Made many scientific observations during his voyage. Also famous as an astronomer and mathematician and the first Greek to put forward a correct theory about the ebb and flow of tides and their relation to the moon.
*See map on page 96*

## SCYLAX
500's B.C.                    Greece
About 510 B.C.: Born in Caryanda in Asia Minor, Scylax was probably a commander in the Persian fleet. He was sent by King Darius I of Persia to explore the course of the Indus River and try to find a sea route from India to Egypt. Sailed down the Indus to the Arabian Sea, across the entrance to the Persian Gulf, around Arabia, and up the Red Sea to Egypt in 2½ years.
*See map on page 93*

## STRABO
63 B.C.( ?)–A.D. 24( ?)       Greece
20 B.C.( ?):Left Amasya, Asia Minor, to live in Rome. Traveled in Europe, Asia, Egypt, and Libya in search of geographical information. Wrote at

least 47 historical books, which are now lost, but 17 volumes of his *Geography* survive.

## SUETONIUS PAULINUS
dates unknown                 Rome
A.D. 42: The first Roman to travel across the Atlas mountains. As consul in Mauretania (now the northern parts of Morocco and Algeria), he led an expedition southward from the Mediterranean coast of North Africa. Crossed the mountains, probably between the high peaks of the Grand Atlas and the Saharan Atlas.
*See map on page 118*

## XENOPHON
434( ?)–355 B.C.( ?)          Greece
401 B.C.: Joined an army of Greek mercenaries under Cyrus to fight King Artaxerxes II of Persia. Marched from Sardis (near modern Izmir in eastern Turkey), through Cilicia into what is now Syria, and down the Euphrates River. After the death of Cyrus in the Battle of Cunaxa, north of Babylon, was elected to lead 10,000 Greek soldiers back to Greece. Marched up the Tigris River to Nineveh, through Kurdestan, Armenia, and Georgia. Reached the Black Sea at Trapezus (Trabzon).
394 B.C.: Retired to Elis, near Olympia in the Peloponnesus, and devoted himself to writing. Wrote philosophical essays and histories, including an account of his expedition with the Ten Thousand.
*See map on page 93*

# Glossary

**Amon-Re:** Chief god of the ancient Egyptians. Originally two gods: Re, the sun god from whom all Egyptian kings claimed descent and whose center of worship was at Heliopolis; and Amon, the sun god worshiped in Thebes. When Thebes became the capital of the Egyptian kings, the two traditions merged and, by about 1525 B.C., Amon had become Amon-Re, the supreme god.

**Asia Minor:** Peninsula of western Asia, bounded on the north by the Black Sea, on the south by the Mediterranean Sea, on the west by the Aegean Sea, and on the east by the Upper Euphrates River. The region is now mainly occupied by Turkey.

**Assyria:** Ancient kingdom on the Upper Tigris River in what is now northern Iraq.

**Baal Shamin:** Carthaginian god at whose temple Hannibal swore eternal enmity for Rome. *Baal* comes from the Phoenician word for a god.

**bematistae:** Scientists (botanists and geographers) who accompanied Alexander the Great on his campaigns. The *bematistae (steppers)* were the road surveyors who counted steps to calculate the distance traveled.

**Caria:** Ancient region of southwest Asia Minor, bounded on the south and southwest by the Aegean Sea, and extending northward to the Maeander River (modern Menderes).

**Dorians:** Invaders into Greece from the north who ended the Mycenaean civilization and plunged Greece into the Dark Ages from about 1100 to 600 B.C.

**dynasty:** Succession of rulers of the same line or family. The Dynastic Period of Egypt (3100–332 B.C.) includes 31 separate dynasties.

**Egypt, Upper and Lower:** Before the Dynastic Period, Egypt was divided into two kingdoms. Lower Egypt consisted of the Nile Delta region; Upper Egypt stretched from Memphis (14 miles south of modern Cairo) to the First Cataract (now in the province of Aswan). The two were united by King Menes, the first ruler of the First Dynasty, in 3100 B.C.

**Homer:** Greek poet, traditionally regarded as the author of the *Iliad* and the *Odyssey*. Homer is generally thought to have lived during the 800's B.C., but nothing is known of his life and some scholars doubt that he ever existed. Others believe that the *Iliad* and the *Odyssey* were not composed by Homer but merely put together from separate poems which were originally recited and not written down. *See also* Iliad, Odyssey

**Iliad:** Epic poem in 24 books, attributed to Homer. The *Iliad* tells the story of the siege of Troy (Ilium) by the Greeks. *See also Homer, Troy*

**Illyria:** Ancient territory on the eastern Adriatic coast of present-day Albania and Yugoslavia.

**Ionians:** One of the main branches of the ancient Greek people. The Ionians were driven from Greece, and settled on the west coast of Asia Minor.

**Macedonia:** District to the north of Ancient Greece. Rose to great importance in the 300's B.C. under Philip II and Alexander the Great.

**Mauretania:** Coastal region of North Africa in what are now the northern parts of Morocco and Algeria.

**Minoans:** People of ancient Crete. Their great legendary ruler was Minos, but this name may have been a title given to all the kings of Crete.

**Nestorians:** Followers of Nestorius, bishop of Constantinople in the A.D. 400's. Nestorius denied that the Virgin Mary was the mother of God, and was excommunicated and banished in A.D. 431. His followers fled beyond the frontiers of the Roman Empire. Today, there are Nestorian Christians in Persia, China, and India.

**Nubia:** Land extending from the First Cataract of the Nile to Meroe, in what is now the Sudan.

**Numidia:** Coastal district of North Africa, now in eastern Algeria.

**Oceanus:** The great outer sea believed by ancient philosophers to surround the whole world.

**Odyssey:** Epic poem ascribed to Homer. The *Odyssey* describes the wanderings of Odysseus, king of Ithaca, on his way home after the fall of Troy. It is in 24 books. *See also Homer, Troy*

**oracle:** Mouthpiece of a god. Strictly, the response of a god to a question asked him by a worshiper, but also applied to the person through whom the god is believed to speak, and to the shrine in which this takes place. The most famous oracles were at Delphi in Greece and Siwah in Egypt.

**Parthians:** Race who conquered the Persians in the 100's B.C. and ruled from the Euphrates to the Indus, with Ecbatana (modern Hamadan in northwestern Iran) as their capital.

**pharaoh:** Name given to the kings of Egypt after 1370 B.C. Originally the word meant *royal palace* but it was gradually applied to the occupant too.

**Pillars of Hercules:** Rocks on either side of the Strait of Gibraltar—the Rock of Gibraltar, and Jebel Musa at Ceuta in North Africa. According to one legend, Hercules set up the two rocks as a warning to sailors not to enter the Atlantic Ocean.

**Ptolemy:** Name of all Egyptian kings belonging to the Greek line. The first was Ptolemy I Soter, one of Alexander the Great's generals.

**Punic Wars:** The three wars between Rome and Carthage (264–241 B.C.; 218–201 B.C.; 149–146 B.C.) which ended with the destruction of Carthage. *Punic* is the Latin word for Phoenician.

**Tartessus:** A region of southwestern Spain near the mouth of the Guadalquivir River.

**Troy:** Also called Ilium. Ancient city in Asia Minor, at the southern end of the Dardanelles. Nine successive Troys were built on the same site (modern Hissarlik in northwestern Turkey) over a period of 3,000 years.

# Index

# Picture Credits

Listed below are the sources of all the illustrations in this book. To identify the source of a particular illustration, first find the relevant page on the diagram opposite. The number in black in the appropriate position on that page refers to the credit as listed below.

1 Aldus Archives
2 Photo Ashmolean Museum, Oxford
3 Barnaby's Picture Library
4 Photo Roloff Beny
5 Courtesy of the Biblioteca Ambrosiana, Milan
6 Biblioteca Mediceo Laurenziana, Florence/Photo Guido Sansoni © Aldus Books
7 Bibliothèque de l'Arsenal, Paris/ Photo R. Lalance © Aldus Books
8 Photo Bibliothèque Nationale, Paris
9 Bibliothèque Nationale et Universitaire, Strasbourg/Photo © Aldus Books
10 Courtesy of the Curators of the Bodleian Library
11 Photo Denise Bourbonnais © Aldus Books
12 Reproduced by courtesy of the Trustees of the British Museum
13 British Museum/Photo John Freeman © Aldus Books
14 British Museum/Photo Michael Jaanus © Aldus Books
15 Courtesy of The Brooklyn Museum, Charles Edwin Wilbour Fund
16 J. Augusta and Z. Burian, Prehistoric Man, Prague
17 Photo by J. Allan Cash
18 Photo Anthony W. Chaffe © Aldus Books
19 Photo Peter Clayton
20 H. Albrecht/Bruce Coleman Ltd.
21 Simon Trevor/Bruce Coleman Ltd.
22 Courtauld Institute of Art, courtesy Lord Leicester
23 Photo J. E. Dayton
24 Department of Archaeology, Pakistan
25 Courtesy Director General of Antiquities, République Libanaise, Beirut
26 C. M. Dixon, London
27 Mary Evans Picture Library

28 Photo W. Forman
29 Geographical Projects Limited, London
30 Painting by Peter Sullivan © Geographical Projects Limited, London, courtesy Mansell Collection
31 Giraudon, Paris
32 Photo George W. Goddard © Aldus Books
33 Photo P. Gotch
34 Government of Hyderabad, Pakistan
35 Reproduced by gracious permission of Her Majesty Queen Elizabeth II/ Photo A. C. Cooper, Ltd.
36 Photo Michael Holford © Aldus Books
37 Michael Holford Library
38 India Office Library and Records
39 Photo André Jodin, Paris
40 Keystone
41 Kunsthistorisches Museum, Wien
42 Redrawing © Aldus Books from Paul Aucler, Carthage, Librairie Delagrave, Paris
43 Mansell Collection
44 The Metropolitan Museum of Art, New York
45 Musée Cernuschi, Paris/Photo Jean-Abel Lavaud © Aldus Books
46 Musée du Louvre, Paris/Photo Denise Bourbonnais © Aldus Books
47 Musée du Louvre, Paris/Photo Service Documentations Photographiques © Aldus Books
48 Museo, Paestum/Photo Scala
49 Museo delle Terme, Roma/Photo Scala
50 Museo Nazionale, Napoli/Photo Scala
51 Museum für Indische Kunst, Staatliche Museen, Preufsischer Kulturbesitz, Berlin-Dahlem
52 Staatliche Museen Stiftung

Preussischer Kulturbesitz, Museum für Ostasiatische Kunst, Berlin
53 Museum of Archaeology, Madrid/ Photo Mas © Aldus Books
54 Chinese and Japanese Special Fund. Courtesy, Museum of Fine Arts, Boston
55 Ross Collection. Museum of Fine Arts, Boston
56 Ny Carlsberg Glyptotek, Copenhagen
57 Bild-Archiv der Österreichischen Nationalbibliothek, Wien
58 Piazza Armerina/Photo Scala
59 Picturepoint, London
60 The Pierpont Morgan Library. M.917 folio 109
61 Josephine Powell, Rome
62 Radio Times Hulton Picture Library
63 Ravenna, S. Vitale/Photo Scala
64 Photo Ann Reading
65 Photo Marshall Cavendish Ltd. reproduced by permission of The Master and Fellows, St. John's College, Cambridge
66 British Crown Copyright. Science Museum, London
67 Secretariat d'Etat aux Affaires Culturelles et a l'Information, Republique Tunisienne, Le Bardo
68 Charles Swithinbank
69 The Tate Gallery, London
70 Sally Anne Thompson
71 U.P.I.
72 From collections of the University Museum of the University of Pennsylvania
73 Courtesy Daniël Van Der Meulen
74 Victoria & Albert Museum, London/ Photo John Freeman © Aldus Books
75 Villa Giulia, Roma
76 Photo C. Woolf © Aldus Books
77 ZEFA
The time chart on pages 180-181 was prepared by Anthea Barker

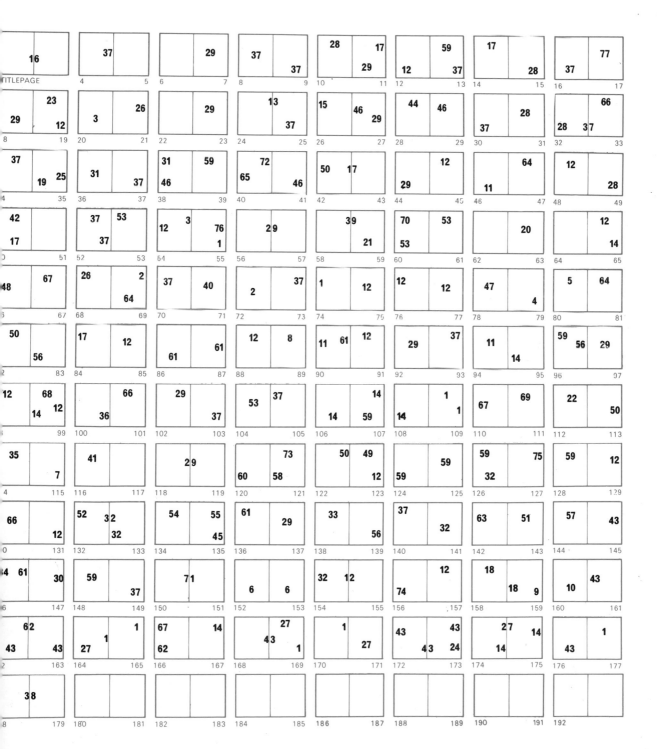